T0123368

THE ELEVENTH COMMANDMENT:
THOU SHALT NOT DEFRAUD THY NATION

EJIKE R. EGWUEKWE

THE ELEVENTH COMMANDMENT:
THOU SHALT NOT DEFRAUD THY NATION

iUniverse books may be ordered through booksellers or by contacting:

iUniverse
1663 Liberty Drive
Bloomington, IN 47403
www.iuniverse.com
1-800-Authors (1-800-288-4677)

ISBN: 978-1-5320-9684-6 (sc)
ISBN: 978-1-5320-9683-9 (e)

Print information available on the last page.

iUniverse rev. date: 03/18/2020

DEDICATED:

To All good leaders of the world (past, present, and future) for their effort and contribution toward making the world a peaceful place for cohabitation through economic, social, and political solidarity. It is a difficult task, but not impossible.

To My parents Mr. and Mrs. Nebife William Egwuekwe for all they have done for me.

To My daughter, Kaosoluchi Egwuekwe; and in memory of my brother, Celestine Egwuekwe, a loving, caring and dynamic gentleman. When you transitioned into eternal life, you took a piece of my heart with you. Safeguard it for me.

AND

To Rev. Fr. (Dr.) Hilary C. Achunike and Rev. Fr. (Dr.) Ndubueze Fabian Mmagu, for their humility, nobleness, kindness of heart, wisdom, and a cosmic degree of understanding. Men of intelligence, honesty, godliness, and deep-rooted integrity.

If the world were filled with people like them, this book would not be necessary.

Thanks be to You, Creator mine,
Whose skilful hands and divinely thoughts
Moulded my frame without a blame.
You gave me a fleeting flame:

That in my span of life, I may go through strife and hate,
Buttressed with hardship, irony, and fate.
Grant that I live to accept my fate with faith;
And that I offer nothing but love and kindness to mankind.
Rescind from me thoughtless prejudice of any sort;

So that I may live to help the weak,
And learn to serve the poor, the needy, the humble, and the meek,
That when Death wins, I should not miss
That Pathway to eternal glory.

ACKNOWLEDGEMENTS

I am fully responsible for all the controversies, if any, that this book may evoke.

While it is not intended for such, I am aware that human nature may arouse some emotions, stir some arguments in favour or against any or all the ideas contained herein. While I am not in the business of trying to please or displease any person or body of persons except saying that which I perceive to be the truth concerning the politico-economic anomalies in our societies, whereof I have given my own suggestions as pertains the remedies, I hereby acknowledge that not everyone will agree with the content thereof.

Some may agree with it in part, some in whole, while others not at all. Some may have better knowledge of the problems and perhaps, also better solutions.

Based on that fact, I welcome criticisms, be they positive or negative, big or small –so long as they are solid, constructive, and challenging – for such could expand by understanding and shed more light in those areas where by knowledge is dim.

I wish to thank the following: Dr. Robert Getz, Professor Emeritus, Political Science Department, State University of New York at Brockport, for the patience he mustered in reading through the manuscript despite his busy schedule.

I am equally indebted to Dr. William Andrews, Professor Emeritus, Political Science Department, SUNY –Brockport, for the advice and encouragement he gave me toward writing this book. Last, but not the least, I will not forget to deliver a basket of gratitude to Dr. Rawle Farley, Professor Emeritus, Department of Economics, SUNY Brockport, for granting me interviews in regards to this writing.

INTRODUCTION

He that has abated and aided in the fleecing of his nation has constantly blamed other and Mother Nature for the untold sufferings bequeathed on his folks and kinsmen. Slavery had come and gone. Scramble, partition and colonization of Africa had come and gone. The wound has healed. But the scar is still there. Its effect is marginally more severe than the original wound. Throughout history, colonialism always left impacts, devious at best, and devastating at worst, on the socio political economy as well as the geopolitics of its former colony. The extent to which an individual nation would allow the evil impact of colonialism to dominate, and influence it - socially, culturally, economically, politically, and otherwise, will determine the extent of the growth of such a nation in any, or all of the social attributes mentioned afore.

Hardly in history is there any nation that had not been colonized at one time or another. It no longer should matter that the nations were colonized. History has been made. It has become an indelible part of the history of those nations and NOTHING can be done about it. The history cannot be changed no matter how much fussing, bickering, economy. What we can do to change the negative economic dimension is to "keep our shoulders high," strive vehemently to achieve the utmost potential any individual nation can achieve. The United States of America was once under the spell of colonialism. It emancipated itself from such shackles, divested itself of the ugly effects of colonialism, moved ahead and carved itself a world of economic and political might. This could not have been so, had the United States folded its hands and fussed, and fussed, and fussed about the evil perpetrated by the colonial master.

What the colonial-master stole from Africa, subjugated Africa to a perpetual economic blitz. There is no doubt about it. However, what is killing Africa today is none other than Africans in conjunction with the white man, stealing whatever is left of the nation. For the life of me, I have never seen, or heard a reversed scenario whereby the white man steals from his country and deposits in the coffer of a black nation. When natural resources and the like keep flowing from one end of the world to other parts of the world without being replenished from ages to ages, coupled with hash climatic conditions, one should not wonder why that part of the world is still in its dark ages.

Africa was the birthplace of man. Civilization started in Africa, yet Africa is still backward; and is referred to as "The dark continent". Africa was endowed with all imaginable natural resources. Africa had the potential of being the most affluent society on earth. It could have been, had it utilized its resources to its beneficial effect. This can still happen, if the fleecing of Africa stops - TODAY, and things get turned around.

African treasure. One does not need to go far to see my point. Listen to the news and see what is happening to the African Elephants in Kenya, diamonds in Sierra Leone, even Artifacts, gold, petroleum, money, from various African nations are being siphoned for onward transmittal to the white man's country. The foregoing is the periphery of the compendium of this book, A kingdom that divides against itself, how can it stand? For the past five centuries or more, things have been flowing from Africa to the western world ranging from slavery to natural resources to money to artifacts, you name it. What makes it worse is that the black man is helping and abating in the fleecing of his own clamouring, and lamenting we make about what the colonial-master did to our nations' Military intervention in civil polity is another issue dealing a devastating blow to political and economic developments of the "new" African nations. It is about time the politicians realized the "reasons" for military come-backs, and get things done right – to stop history from repeating itself. The contemporary African politicians had been beaten once, and a second, and a third, by the military. The maxim that comes to mind here is, "once beaten, twice, shy. Thus, it is about time our politicians got things done right – so the military would not have any excuse to interfere with the existing political order.

❖ In this book, the name or names of a nation or body of nations are often times used.

Where it so applies, it does not mean I intend to single out such nation or nations. I only used such to illustrate my points.

❖ Although the phrase "Thou Shalt Not Defraud Thy Nation" in the context of this book centripetally refers to Africa and its peoples, centrifugally it encompasses all nations of the world and its peoples. For, no nation should be defrauded.

❖ Wherever the word "our" or "ours" is used in this book, it first refers to all persons of color for Africa is their continent. Second, it refers to all human beings, for Africa being the birthplace of man, is our collective responsibility to rebuild – not destroy.

PART 1

The Part to Political Stability

CHAPTER ONE

Roots of Political Instability

*Take a look at the map of Africa. You will notice that its
contour represents a shape which reminds one of a ham-
bone. To some people this ham-bone has been designed by
destiny for the carving knife of European imperialism; to
others, it is a question mark which asks whether Europe
will live up to its ethical profession of peace and harmony.
Yet the paradox of Africa is that its wealth and resources
are among the root causes of wars. Since the Berlin
Conference, the continent of Africa has been partitioned
and dominated by armies of occupation in the guise of
political trustees and guardians...*[1]

-Nnamdi Azikiwe

Of all the five continents of the world Africa is the most politically
unstable. This problem has gone on from decade to decade and has
eaten deep into the fabric of Africa's socio-political existence; and the
end is not yet in sight. Africa was not created with political instability.
As a matter of fact, before the advent of colonialism, Africa was known
to have had a cohesive political base, in its own style. For example, as far
back as 384 B.C., Upper Libya[2] had a solid, workable political structure
as recognized by Aristotle. During the nineteenth century, Sokoto
(Nigeria), under the leadership of Usman dan Fodio, had a vanguard

of military and political strength, and a "good government over a wide area, leading to the expansion of trade."[3]

Also, as far back as 400 A.D., "the kingdoms of the Western Sudan -Ghana, Mali, Songhay – were remarkable in the degree to which they were able to establish complex political structures that centralized the government of large areas of West Africa. Political superiority here, as often elsewhere, was based on a technological advantage."[4]

Thus, Africa was not without solid political management, nor were they lacking in areas of technology before the Western influence.

Therefore, the political problems in Africa today could be seen as a hangover of the after effects of colonialism. To find solutions to the problems, one has to first study the problems. In analyzing the problems, one finds that they originate from two distinct, but related, facets. While one has a remote colonial connection, the other is tied to the existing political organizations, be they civil or military, democratic or totalitarian, oligarchic or dictatorial. Thus, the extent to which political stability is achieved in a nation depends more on internal, than external, factors. For example, a popular government can command a greater respect and allegiance of its people than an unpopular one.

As the political malaise are said to have had a distant colonial rooting, the problems may not be fully understood without a historical overview of colonialism and its effects on that continent.

As early as 1434, Alonzo Gonzales and his fellow Portuguese merchants had identified Africans as a good commodity for slavery. Soon after, the Spaniards and the Dutch joined. Then followed by the French and the English, respectively. The trade was of immense boom to the traffickers. Their plantations, agriculture, service and industry were at the peak of production with slave labor. The most devastating aspect of the trade is that children of Africa are scattered all over the face of the earth via slavery; the evidence of which can be seen in every nook and cranny of the world. This was the beginning of the debasing of Africa. Heretofore, it has not recovered from the loss of human resources on account of the trade, even as we enter the Twenty-first century.

A passive observer may argue that five-hundred years of lapse is enough for the continent to recover from the losses resulting from slavery. One should bear in mind that the loss of human resources is an irrecoverable loss. The Vacuum created can never be filled. The legitimate question to ask here is, what can be done (to recover some degree of the losses, and/or) to stop further losses of any kind from occurring? Some notable blacks such as Henry Sylvester Williams, Marcus Garvey, George Padmore, and W. E. B. DuBois, devised their own solution in an effort to redress the problems facing the black man in their day. Their ideas of the solution varied, ranging from 'Back-To Africa' movement to demand for total and unconditional restitution, none of which is effectively applicable to today's problems in the political-economic arena of the African continent.

Theirs was a dream centered on the unification of blacks, and a fervent effort to wipe out the humiliations suffered by blacks for the past five hundred years.

The problem they were out to solve was that of racism. Their inclination could be summed up in Stanley Allen's words, for their effort "presents in one sense the Negro African poet's endeavour to recover for his race a normal self-pride, a lost confidence in himself, a world in which he again has a sense of identity and a significant role."[5] Racialism is still alive and well. It is still practiced in the metropolitan countries even as we march into the Twenty-first century. The burning-down of more than one hundred and fifty black churches in the South and Southwest of the United States between January 1995 and June 1997, in a case in point. Also, the experience one encounters in churches, as whites tend to avoid seating on the same pew occupied by a black fellow, is an indication that as those notable personalities did not solve the race issue, a genius has not been bora who could. The problems between whites and the African race have never dissipated, but rather have exacerbated in other directions.

The debasement of Africa did not end with slavery. No sooner had the trade been abolished, than the merchants found a new exploitative way (colonialism) to replace the abolished trade. From late nineteenth-century, colonialism started and like the slave trade, quickly gathered momentum. With the exception of Liberia which was an American creation, the whole of West Africa was scrambled, partitioned, and colonized from about 1885. Responsible government started to emerge in Africa around 1951, notably in Nigeria and Ghana. Other African nations soon after followed suit in determining self-rule, thus, ending five-hundred-years of direct European exploitation of the continent. It could not be said that the colonialists were willing to relinquish their acquisition of the colonies. They only did so for they had no choice. The nationalists, who were alumni of European and American education, had become African patriots soon after their realization of the colonial exploitation. The colonialists understood this, as well as the economic mess they had dragged the continent into, and that they had not much interest left by hanging on.

Colonialism had a devious effect on the continent and its people. One of its evil attributes was not paying heed to the differences in the language and culture of the various peoples of Africa before lumping them into one nation or another. For example, the peoples of Nigeria comprise a plural society with nearly 250 distinct languages. The peoples' cultures are also distinct. Thus, the peoples, their languages and cultures, are completely different from each other. Without giving regard to these obvious differences, the peoples of Nigeria were politically lumped together and the area was christened "Nigeria" (coined from the words: Niger - Area, by Flora Shaw, who later became the wife of lord Lugard). There is no denying the fact that such differences do play a major role in the political unstableness of the area.

Differences in language and culture for one thing do promote fear, mistrust and suspicion. Such problems accentuate ethnocentrism which in turn creates nepotism and favoritism, as each tribe would prefer to deal with its own people at the detriment of others. As will later be discussed, such differences and the problems associated with them could be seen as the major reason for the collapse of Nigeria in the first republic.

However, it did not matter to the white man what the differences were. What mattered to him was to divide, rule, and exploit. For example, from 1944 through 1968, more than fifty Western companies came to Liberia, "mainly to exploit Liberia's mineral resources."[6] Liberia was then Africa's largest producer of Iron-ore and the third largest in the world following Sweden and Venezuela. An American firm called the Liberian Mining Company was established to make such exploits. On yearly bases, it exported 20 million tons of Iron-ore from Liberia alone. When the American firm (Liberian Mining Company) closed down in 1977, it left "nothing behind but huge holes in the ground. Also, between 1923 and 1964 the British government collected 40 million pounds in taxes in Northern Rhodesia but spent only 5 million pounds on development."[7]

Besides mineral resources, there was an abundance of cash crops, which the colonialists also laid their hands upon. Much as they did in mining, they equally did on cash crops. Almost every territory had some cash crop of some value or another. There was wine in Algeria, cocoa in Nigeria and Ghana, cotton in Uganda and Sudan, coffee in Ivory Coast, Tobacco in Southern Rhodesia, and sisal in Tanganyika.

The metropolitan powers merely extracted these wealth of fortune and expatriated same to their metropolitan base. They were not interested in solidifying the African social base, nor were they interested in strengthening the political structure. All they cared about was EXPLOITATION.

It suffices to say that the revenues collected from such exploits were siphoned and/or transferred overseas to the white man's land and was not in any way, shape or form, used in the development of Africa; nor was it used to prepare the new nations for self-governance. For instance in the Congo, till the date of its independence, Belgian group of companies, controlled all the mineral resources in that country: copper, cobalt, diamond, uranium, cadmium, silver, tungsten, columbium and platinum. Between 1950 and 1959, net profits of 620 million dollars were made by the Belgian Société group.

During this time, the overall mining of these minerals increased by 149 per cent, and the pre-independence domestic product totalled over a billion dollars, half of which went to foreign firms and resident expatriates. None of this money went toward the development of the Congo.

Although such massive exploitation committed by the colonialist was done many decades ago, the impact is still being felt in two dimensions: one is that the minerals extracted from these areas may never be replenished nor could the money siphoned be retrieved. The other is that the black man is sheepishly following the same footstep of the colonialist. It is understandable, though morally wrong, that the colonialist stole all he could from Africa and used the proceeds to develop his own nation. What boggles the mind and is difficult to understand is, the black man continuing where the white man left off in defrauding his own nation, and in tandem transfers the proceeds also to the white man's country. This re-visitation of exploitation (this time around done by the Africans) is the last straw. A kingdom that defrauds itself cannot stand.

From the trend of such continuous transfer of resources, one could extrapolate that theworst economic woes is in the offing within the continent of Africa. However, as the world is becoming more and more shrunk, all the continents are becoming more and more interdependent – none can do without the other –no matter how minimal a contact. Thus, fleecing a continent at the detriment of its people is not that much of a wise move.

The economic and socio-political discomfort created by such transfer will, directly or indirectly, be felt even by those that benefited from the exploitation. For instance, such discomfort could create an influx of people from the economically depressed nations to the more affluent ones (as will be discussed in Chapter Ten). This alone, has its own cycle of social ills such as decrease in population in the one and increase in population in the other. (This will be descanted in Chapter Ten).

Another source of political instability in Africa is the introduction of the Western political order. The Western political systems - Democracy, Socialism, Communism, Feudalism and all the other –isms with their political ramifications were totally unknown to the African before the advent of the colonial empire nor did the colonialists care enough to guide the new emerging African nations through the Western political structure; nor was the African taught how the system works. The new nations were left to fend for themselves politically and economically after the massive exploitation. Had the new nations been schooled on the workings of the political systems during the colonial era, or at least before the attainment of independence, ours could have been a politically stable continent. This is one of the principal reasons for the political instability that still sweeps through the length and breadth of the African continent. The depth of Africa's political problems may not be fully understood without a historical overview of colonialism and its impacts.

CHAPTER TWO

Colonialism and its Effects

The white man came to Africa with the Bible in one hand and the sword in the other. While the black man, with his eyes closed, was busy embracing the new religion, the white man through colonialism, dug out the existing mineral resources. By the time the Africans stirred from the slumber and opened their eyes, in late 50s and early 60s, their resources were gone. They had been robbed blind. With the same sword, through religious means, he destroyed the traditional religion, and struck a nerve of confusion and disbelief in the people as regards their traditional system of inter-personal identification with the Supreme Being. The Africans still half awake, or half asleep, take-over from where the colonialists stopped, and rob, and rob, and rob their own nations blind. But they don't even realize they are inimically robbing themselves.

Since after the advent of the missionaries and the subsequent emergence of the colonial rule which started from about 1885 to about 1951, Africa has never been the same socially, culturally, economically, politically and otherwise. Soon after the Berlin conference of European powers in 1884, European soldiers set out to scramble, partition, and colonize Africa. Depending on how one looks at it, the early missionaries and the colonialists were one and the same albeit with different faces. While one can argue that the missionaries came to Africa for the purpose of bringing Christianity to Africa, one may not be far from the truth to assert that the missionaries' presence paved the way and facilitated colonialism.

This statement can be qualified in many ways which will be seen both in this chapter and the subsequent ones. In their effort to persuade slave-dealers to end the trade, the abolitionists most of which were Christians who had visited Africa, had advised that "an inexhaustible mine of wealth is neglected in Africa, for the prosecution of this impious traffic; that if proper measures were taken, the revenue of this country might be greatly improved, its naval strength increased, its colonies in a more flourishing situation, the planters richer, and a trade, which is now a source of blood and desolation, converted into one which might be prosecuted with advantage and honor."[8]

However, it would be a judgment rippled with fallacy, to equate the work of the early missionaries with the rip-offs perpetrated by the colonialists. While the one was more involved in increasing the number of its converts, the other was engaged in aggrandizing the wealth of their 'mother'-country.

Though the assertion cited above may have been made by the abolitionists with no diabolical intentions, that assertion is still culpable as to the effect it had on attracting an influx of colonizers into Africa. That the missionaries and the colonizers were an extension of each other cannot be overemphasized neither could it be doubted. For example, in 1738, Jacobus Eliza Capitein, an ex- slave from the Gold Coast studying in the University of Leiden, confirmed "that slavery was not incompatible with Christianity and could indeed be its instrument."[9]

But, after seeing the ugly side of slavery and the miseries inflicted on the slaves, the Christians repudiated the trade as could be noted when in 1749, or thereabouts, Bishop Bartholomew de la Casas remonstrated the King of Spain that he would suffer the loss of his soul if he did not detour from the nefarious act of slavery. Though the king was touched by the remonstrance, he was more concerned with magnifying his economic gains than in worrying about the Judgment Day. The effort of the missionaries toward the abolition of slavery was a near-flop in the beginning as was seen in Spain. The effort came to fruition after a great deal of persistence. It could be equally argued that the effort of the missionaries were not enough in stopping the slave trade. Britain may have banned the trade simply because it had gotten enough slaves to engage in Agriculture and other domestic chores. Or perhaps Britain agreed to the stoppage because it was already beginning to experience difficulties with the many number of slaves imported to England. This could be deduced from the statement of Sir John Fielding in 1780, worried about the continuous increase of slaves and the social problems they were perceived to be creating, talking about the slaves, he said:

They no sooner arrive here than they put themselves on a footing with other servants, become intoxicated with liberty, grow refractory, and either by persuasion of others or from their own inclinations, begin to expect wages according to their own opinion of their merits; and as there are already a great number of black men and women who have made themselves so troublesome and dangerous to the families who have brought them over to get themselves discharged, these enter into societies and make it their business to corrupt and dissatisfy the mind of every black servant that comes to England; first by getting them christened or married, which, they inform them, makes them free... though it has not been decided otherwise by the judges. However, it so far answers their purpose that it gets the mob on their side and makes it not only difficult but dangerous...to recover possession of them... indeed, it is the less evil of thetwo to let them go about their business, for there is great reason that those blacks who have been sent back to the plantations have been the occasion of those... recent insurrections...[10]

Sir John Fielding's statement supports the argument that Britain may have agreed to stop the vice because of the looming problems. Be that as it may, whether the abolition of the trade came to a conclusive reality simply because Britain conceded to it or not, the important role played by the missionaries towards its eventual stoppage cannot be underestimated. Since after detecting the evil nature of the trade, the missionaries continued to preach and harangue against it. "In 1754, the religious Society of Friends solemnly declared that 'to live in ease and plenty by the toil of those whom fraud and violence had put into their power, was neither consistent with Christianity nor common justice'... to possess a little in an honourable way, was better than to possess much through the medium of injustice."[11] Thus, the missionaries disavowed slavery.

At this juncture one may pause to wonder, if the missionaries had renounced other forms of exploitation of Africa as they did of slavery, couldn't the exploitation have stopped much earlier; and could Africa have been exploited as much as it was? Or perhaps the missionaries being anxious to end the cruelty imposed by slavery merely happily sang Hallelujah, Gloria in excelsis Deo, for their success in bringing that aspect of vice to a close. They did not attempt to stop the economic part of the exploitation.

Perhaps they encouraged it in place of the abolished trade? Whatever may be the answer to these questions, it should be reckoned that without the relentlessness of the missionaries to effectuate the abolition of the trade, the dealers perhaps would not have minded siphoning the entire peoples of the continent into slavery. The European dealers had insisted that should the Africans have the desire to sell their sons and daughters into slavery, they should have the desire to buy them.

On the same footing, the African suppliers were reluctant to do away with the business too. An example of such reluctance could be deduced from the "story of a chief in the Niger delta, who when exhorted to sell elephant tusks instead of men replied with more wit than humanity that it was far easier to catch a man than an elephant."[12] Slavery, therefore, was a means of easy cash.

Besides, slaves were like personal possessions and properties that could be destroyed at the whims of the owner. Many were killed. Many were lynched. And many were thrown into the sea en-route. With this in mind, it would be a marginal error to underrate the role of the missionaries by displacing it with the argument that Britain stopped slavery because it was saturated with same.

It should be mentioned in passing here that Africa had almost always been associated with slavery, albeit falsely. Although slavery ended with Africa, it did not start from there. Slavery was as old as human existence. The Old Testament of the Bible made mention of Israelites in bondage in Egypt. The Old Roman Empire was built by slave labour; and perhaps, so was the Old Greek Empire. Slavery is therefore, not synonymous with Africa. With this in mind, the aforesaid European dealers should have been wiser to look in their neighbourhood for those desirous of selling their children for which they should have contented themselves on buying, rather than look on faraway Africa for that which have been easily obtained in their own backyards.

Another area in which the western influence impacted the society was culture in regards to the peoples' religion. In the Igboland of Nigeria, when the early missionaries came, they saw the Africans as heathens and/or pagans. The former connotes: either worshipper of idols or one who did not worship the Almighty God, and the latter implied people without religion. In the first place, these two names given to the Africans on arrival were as misleading as they were erroneous. Secondly, they were contradictory one unto the other.

I will defend the latter before the former as the ignorance of the day calls for prompt illumination on such appellation. The people were seen as worshippers of idols and at the same time accused of not having any religion. If this is not a contradiction unto itself, then nothing else is. A worshipper of idol was a worshipper of something and as such, had a religion. When analyzed more critically, even the notion that the African was worshipping idols was also false. Before the European influence, cameras were unknown in Africa. The Africans of the day therefore, did not have any form of retaining the memorabilia of those of their ancestors who, in their own imagination, had led a good life.

The only choice they had was to carve memorabilia in form of images, with which to remember their holy ancestors. Those who were perceived to have led diabolical lives were never remembered. Also, the people had a strong affirmation in the existence of the Almighty God, whom they had always referred to as Chi-ukwu (the Big God). Before the European influence, the people also knew that they were created by God, as they referred to Him as Chineke (God the Creator); Obasi-Igwe, or Olisa, or Chukwu abiama, or Chiukwu-ukpabi (God of Heaven). In all cultures and among all peoples of the world, the same basic knowledge of the existence of the Mighty-One applies. When studied very analytically, one realizes that, the same cardinal principles, both in concept and epithet, apply. While there may be differences in methods of supplication, which by way of cultural differences there should be, the Jewish God or the Muslim God or the Hindu God or the Buddhist God, or the Christian God, (was not and) is not different from that worshipped by the Africans, both in ancient and modern times. It would be a fallacy, rippled with ignorance, to believe otherwise.

Therefore, there should not be any iota of doubt that the Africans had been very religious and had been firm believers in the existence of God before the advent of Christianity. Much like the Church believes in Angels and Saints as the Messengers of God, the ancient Africans believed in the existence of their holy ancestors and the good demi-gods or minor deities serving as messengers to the Big God. Thus, the purpose of intercession through the Angels and Saints is equivalent to the ancient Africans' intercession through their holy ancestors and the minor deities.

Expressed in a simpler logic, the good African ancestors and the demi-gods were perceived of same equipollence as the Church's (notion of) saints and angels; therefore, the intercessions made either by the ancient Africans through their primogenitors and deities, or the ones made by the modern Church through its angels and saints, in my opinion, have the same equipollency before the eyes of God. The same also is the case with the South America's syncretism and any other religion or medium of worship wherein the ultimate C aim of the supplicant is to communicate with the Almighty God.

Christology and its doctrines may have been a novelty to Africans, the newness of such faith and its acceptance did not mean the people were without religion before its introduction; nor did it mean they did not know God. To believe otherwise is a proof of not only myopia of the mind, but of mental retardation.

As mentioned before, in Africa, as elsewhere, the knowledge of the existence of God was with the people before the emergence of Christendom. Amongst the Akran people of Ghana, for instance, God was (and is still) known and called *Onyankopon* or *Nyankopon* (He who bears the weight of others without crooking). Amongst the Fantis, also of Ghana, the ancestors named God *Twereduampon* (He, who you can lean-on with confidence, for He does not break or bend). God was, and still is, referred to as *Otumfuo* the mightiest and most powerful one); *Odomankoma* (Creator, same as the Igbo word - *Chineke*). Thus, is would not be sacrilegious to brand the missionaries ignorant for their pathetic assumption which gave birth to the aforesaid appellations: heathens, and pagans.

Those that gave those false names had at the same time forgotten or completely and blindly failed to observe that what they saw as idols were a replica of the statues, pictures, portraits, and crucifixes of the "Holy ones" as believed in the Christian doctrine, albeit in African fashion, as their only way of remembering their own "holy ancestors". Similarly, as the Church in its Holiness calls upon the names of Angels and Saints during Religious ceremonies, so did our forefathers in their own tradition, call upon the names of their own holy ones during their own religious ceremonies. The missionaries in their palpable wittiness should have been able to observe the similarities between that which was in practice and the tenet of their own system; and should have made adjustments accordingly, rather than condemning what they did not understand, and did not care to understand, branding it evil.

I would be making the same blind mistake as did the early missionaries, to jump to conclusion and state a priori, that there were non-godly people in Africa. Though such could have been found hither and thither, the number, nevertheless, must have been insignificant. Besides, the ungodly is ubiquitous; and can be found in any nation. There are atheists, agnostics, and even satanists. While the latter is still known to be practiced by few in the western countries of Europe and North America, it is unheard of, and perhaps never even existed in Africa. That which the missionaries saw in Africa and promptly condemned as evil was in existence in Europe during- the same time. For instance, the ancient Greek and Roman empires were known to have had more gods than all the world's combined.

(These were some of their deities: Achilles, Aeollo, Apollo, Amphitrite Ares, Artemis, Bacchus, Calliope, Celeno, Cerberus, Ceres, Charon, Demeter, Diana, Doris, Doto, Erato, Euterpe, Fauna, Faunus,

Galateia, Ganymede, Gorgon, Harpy, Hebe, Hera, Hercules, Hydra, Juno, Jupiter, Jupiter-Pluvius, Laocoon, Leto, Mars, Melpomene, Mercury, Minotaur, Mnemosyne, Neptune, Nereid, Nereus, Niobe, Ocypete, Ops, Pallas Athena, Pan, Pluto, Poseidon, Proserpine, Rhea, Saturn, Terpsichore, Thetis, Zeus, etc.)

The condemnation of African pantheons was sanctimonious. It was a divisive schism to wreck families. Following the same colonial philosophy of divide and rule, the early missionaries had taught the African to disavow all reverence to their ancestors, making them believe that doing so was evil. It suffices here, to mention that, the African following the true sense of his religion was not worshipping his ancestors any more than a true Christian obeys the Commandment: Honor they father and they mother. In addition to this "Honor", however, the African beckons his ancestors (i.e. fathers and forefathers, mothers and foremothers etc.) to join in supplication to none other than the Almighty God; in no less an honorable fashion than a Christian would, in church services. Although the two methods of supplication (Christian and Traditional) vary, as they ought to, the services (one way or another) culminate in Thanks Giving to the Almighty, for blessings received; or in asking for some favours.

Be that as it may, the disavowal of African Traditional religion has had an indelible impact on the African, Directly or indirectly, knowingly or unknowingly, that philosophy created a rift between those who tenaciously held unto the traditional religion and those who succumbed to the new faith. There were instances of those who, following the same school of thought, openly condemned their inconvertible parents or relatives, calling them (not only pagans, but) devils. It suffices to say that if one's parents are devils, then one is a child of the devil. To drum this message home to the African, a myth was introduced portraying the Devil as a black man (with a tail and two horns), while God, His Angels and Saints are portrayed to be white people. This had an effect even on me.

When I was a child, about five years old, I was so perplexed by the pictures I saw in our house, at the churches and at other public places. The pictures always, always had God, Jesus Christ, Angels, and all the

Saints portrayed as white people. The one that had the most disturbing effect on me was the one whereby Angel Michael (white) was with a sword, slaying the Lucifer (black). Then, to add more fuel to the flame of my perplexity, I had noticed two pictures hanging on the wall of a neighbour. One was the picture of Saint Anthony of Padua, while the other was the picture of Saint Claire (both of which were, as usual, whites).

Then, with the innocence of a perplexed child, I went to the 'Block Rosary Crusade', and asked the crusade leaders (who were blacks and whose names were, paradoxically - Anthony, Michael, and Raphael): Do black people go to Heaven? If they do, why don't they have portraits?

My questions were never answered. Perhaps they did not know the answers themselves. Whatever may have been their reasons for not answering, they merely dismissed my questions as those of an over-inquisitive child. However, their refusal to illuminate my young mind threw me into a greater ambiance of perplexity. But inquisitive minds never die, nor do they ever rest. Mine didn't. I wanted an answer. Nevertheless, I dared not ask any other adult: if "the (religious) leaders" didn't know or didn't want to answer, perhaps, no one else would.

In the end, I found an answer within myself. It was though a child's answer to a mythical question. I concluded that maybe black people go to heaven too. Maybe, when black people die, God changed their souls to be white so as to look like God since He created man's soul in His image and likeness. Thus my thinking was, if God were white, He might be changing every holy soul to look like Him. Then, I started collecting as many of the Holy pictures as I could ever find (they were all whites, of course): thinking, when I die my soul would transform into one of those.

My young inquisitive mind did not atrophy at that stage. Much like me, it has grown into adulthood, and has since found an answer to the dismissed questions.

Although Misters Michael and Raphael (the nicest of all the persons I have ever known) have gone to their Maker (as a result of the Nigeria-Biafra civil war), I would discourse my new-found answer with them when, and if, I meet with them in the life to come. And to Mr.

Anthony I here say: Yes. The black people go to Heaven. God does not transform anybody's soul from one race to another upon death.

As a matter of fact, my inquisitive mind has another question, this time to the people depicting God as a white man: Where did they see God? When? How? And on what occasion? If they never saw Him, from whence did they draw their conclusion that God is white?

In the same vein, where did they see Angels Gabriel and Michael (both portrayed as whites), one taking a message from God to the Blessed Virgin Mary, while the other was slaying the ominous (black) Lucifer? Were they eye-witnesses to such accounts?

Were they there when such happened? If not, then, from where and how did they obtain their fallacious notion concerning those invisible Deities? Did they ever see the Lucifer? If not, where did they get their nefarious idea from, as to portray the Devil in a black image?

By the way, who has a more diabolical persona: the one who defaces God's creation, or the one who has been defaced throughout history, for no justifiable cause?

Well, another response I have for my friend, Anthony, is that, the early missionaries, in cohort with the colonialists, used such nebulous myths to inculcate the spirit of inferiority (complex) in the African. Fortunately for them, and unfortunately for the African, it worked.

Now, let us go back to the ignominious allegation that the African had no religion, worshipping idols, worshipping the Devil, and worshipping their ancestors (well, I have made my stance clear in such unfounded and despicable concept).

The same religious shenanigan was used by Spain and Portugal against the Native Indians in Latin America. The people were said to have had no religion. They were branded evil. Inferiority complex was introduced amongst them. They were subjugate and subjected to slave labor and made to pay weighty tributes in order to be taught "Christianity". On occasion, at least hundreds of thousands were killed by those who claimed to be Christians. In my honest opinion, a Christian does not kill physically, psychologically, politically, economically, emotionally, mentally, or otherwise.

If they really were Christians, didn't their Bible contain the Seventh

17

Commandment: Thou Shalt Not Kill? Didn't their Bible contain Jesus' Command: Go ye and teach all nations. If they refuse, wipe off the sand from the soul of your feet, and leave that nation alone?

> *Verbatim et literatim*, a Christian is a Christ's follower. Byimplication, followers should abide by the teachings of the Master whose doctrine they claim to profess. Jesus did not say: wipe off the people, but wipe off the dust from the soul of your feet; which means: Be gone!

The same fate befell some of the African ancestors who refused to abdicate their traditional religious credo, although, not as much as occurred amongst the Native Indians, perhaps, because the Africans did not resist as much as (or put up a fight as did) the Native Indians.

While some modern African Christians may not indulge in physical killings of non converts as did the early missionaries, they are more akin to indulge in psychological, mental, and emotional killings of people who refuse to accept their religious doctrines. In many African societies today, people are yet sceptical about interfaith marriages. In some of these societies, people have the tendency to ostracize, and have little or nothing to do with, those who do not belong in the same religious affiliation as they. Ostracism of a fellow human being based on such religious tenets is the very definition of psychological, mental, or emotional killing. A true Christian (or any true believer of any true religion with any moral foundation) should not kill in whatever ramification of that word.

Another significance of that legacy is that, till today a majority of Africans believe it is sinful to pay any sort of reverence to their ancestors. Some have even gone to the stage of burning and/or destroying the ancestral memorabilia, believing those to be evil. This is not only iconoclastic, it is sacrilegious. Above all, it is foolishness accentuated with ignorance. Whoever indulges in such iconoclastic and sacrilegious acts, deserves some pity, especially from our ancestors whose images are being defamed and defaced. This has caused some mental and psychological, and even in some cases outright physical harm to the iconoclasts. Some were known to have been rendered barren or impotent. Some families were even known to have been wiped out, or rendered useless due to the ancestral wrath or vengeance for the atrocities inveighed upon the ancestral images. Our holy ancestors should be asked for mercy. For this, I ask: fathers, forgive them for they know not what they do.

The irony is that the same white man who sanctimoniously condemned the ancestral images, are the same ones buying them. There arises a question: if those ancestral artifacts were seen as paganish, devilish or Satanic while in Africa, by what means did they get cleansed, thereby making them worthy to be purchased by he who originally condemned them? If they should be good to be taken to the West or East as antiques, what is wrong with their being kept in the national museums or archives; or in the Obi (i.e., family parlor) where they originated from? While they serve as good antiques to the white man, they are still perceived as evil (omen) by the Africans who should have known hotter. If what is good for the goose is not good for the gander, I wonder what is. If one trashes one's national treasure, those that know the value will use it to their advantage. As in the slave situation, an argument can be postulated here: if the Africans are desirous of selling their national ancestral memorabilia as trash, shouldn't the westerners have the right to buy them as treasure?

It must be borne in mind that cameras were unknown to the Africans of the day, until the western influence. In effect, the only choice our forefathers had was to carve images of their loved ones who they believed led a good life while on earth. Thus, only the good, holy ones were remembered. Those who were perceived to have led a bad life were not remembered, nor were they made mention of after their death. The images therefore, were a symbol of holiness, referred to as *Ikenga* or *Okpensi*. The idea behind those images was no different than what is obtainable in modern religion. Much like the church uses crucifixes, pictures, images and/or statues to remember the Angels and Saints who are believed to be Holy, the Africans of old, used the *Ikenga* in remembering their own holy ancestors. It was the only way they knew. Therefore, to the African of old, the prayers conveyed through the

Ikenga had the same degree and effect both in strength and magnitude as that done by modern religionists through their respective modern mediums.

It is a paradox that the Europeans in their fetish desire to eradicate that which they wrongly condemned as evil, had myopically failed to see the existence of pantheons in Europe. It is also perplexing how they had failed to observe the similarities between the so-called new faith and that which was functioning in the society on their arrival. Perhaps they noticed the obvious similarities, yet were bent on catalyzing the people through their sanctimonious philosophy of condemnation. Whatever the case may be, they sullied the society and the impact is still at work in that continent.

Destruction of holy images is not my idea of societal-moral and spiritual purification. There is nothing wrong with following a religion or a defined way of life, but doing it blindly is nothing short of foolishness. Until a people learn to preserve and treasure what they have, that society is in trouble but doesn't even know it. Such a society is a long way from recovery.

Another aspects of the culture greatly affected by European influence are language and marriage. Before the Western influence African languages could be spoken smoothly without corruption. Such is no longer the case. For instance, it is now difficult to find an Igbo person who could speak the Igbo-language fluently without interjecting the English-language in parchments, spattered within the speech. This they call *Engligbo* (a mixture of the two languages).

Much so, Polygyny used to be an acceptable practice in the society. Now it is frowned at. Monogamy has become the norm. It must be mentioned that nowhere in the Bible, or in the Koran, or in the Book of Mormon, was Polygyny condemned. While the Bible may have made mention of 'a man...taking a woman of his choice...and the two become one', it did not specifically denounce Polygyny. For one thing, many of the Holy ones, as believed in the Old Testament of the Bible, such as Abraham, Jacob, Solomon, and David were known to be polygynous (or polygamous). That did not prevent the Almighty from identifying with them. Nor did it make Him hesitate in choosing

David's lineage as where the Messiah should come from. During His time, Jesus Christ had more important things to occupy Himself with than preaching in favour of, or against Polygyny. If for anything, He advocated 'Unification' through His doctrine: "Love thy neighbor as thyself." The idea of making monogamy the only allowable and/or acceptable matrimonial practice in the Christian doctrine developed under Pope Leo XIII and was supported by St. Bonaventure, St. Thomas, Cajetan, and Alexander of Hales, all Catholics. Martin Luther was not a proponent of that doctrine.

The implication of the above is that monogamist doctrine has had a firm grip on the people; and has revolutionized their concept and perception in relation to marriage. The principle of 'One man, One wife', has significantly reduced the number of those who could have taken to marriage. To be Unmarried used to be frowned at; and was seen as 'something bad.' But now, because of the increase in the number of the unmarried, solitary life as well as celibacy have become acceptable phenomena in contemporary Africa. By the same token, divorce, and single parenthood are beginning to emerge, albeit slowly; all as a result of western influence. "The practice of religion is of course not the whole of life. It is needful that religion should not be allowed to make undue havoc of areas of life adjacent and complementary to it, patterns of life which belong to the political economy."[13]

However hard it may be to believe, religion plays an important, if not a dominant, role in Africa's national politics especially in countries where Muslims and Christians are found in substantial proportions. In such places, sometimes, it is as difficult to form a coalition government as it is to reach consensus on issues of national interest. Kaleidoscopically, European influence in Africa was not completely negative. It came with some advantages such as replacing bush-paths with motorable roads. For instance, in Nigeria some old bush-paths which people had used for centuries were replaced by motorable roads. By 1912, motor vehicles could travel from Benin to Asaba, Onitsha, and Udi. Railways were also introduced.

The introduction of certain media of communication such as telephone and telegraph, were also derived from European influence.

On the same account, scientific hospitals, maternity homes and healthcare centers were built to replace the existing unpurified native ones usually run on traditional rudimentary fashion. In line with this, schools were built in Christian areas, while the already existing ones in Muslim areas got uplifted. Also, because of European influence, the standard of living was improved. The foregoing no doubt impacted the people's regular modus Vivendi, and positively changed their life forever.

Looking at it from a more critical standpoint, however, one may argue that those social amenities were introduced, to make life more comfortable for the metropolitan administrators. In other words, the colonizers were not in Africa for the health of Africa; nor were those social goodies introduced because of the colonizers' love for Africa. I have, I believe, made that point clear. But ex *abundanti cautela*, it may suffice to add that the social goodies where a subset of egoistic altruism exemplified by Adam Smith's theory that by pursuing economic self-interests, every individual unconsciously promotes at the same time the economic interests of others. Thus by implication, the amenities were introduced to make life more comfortable for the metropolitan administrators. That Africans benefited from such was merely derivative. If, on the other hand, the colonialists selflessly did so, the introduction then, perhaps, was a colourful way to mislead the people and give them the impression that something was being done for them; thus, to soften their minds, and make them accept colonialism as something good. In which case it could be seen as a decoy. The truth of this could be drawn when a comparison is made between what was taken versus what was provided. Whatever the case may be, the amenities were introduced, and the community benefited.

The positive influence of colonialism notwithstanding, that era is still referred to as "a period when the colonial powers regarded their.. African territories as their 'possessions' existing mainly for the economic, social and political welfare of the 'mother' country …a period of economic exploitation and of political and social humiliation of the peoples of…Africa"[14] All these colonial attributes are still at work in contemporary African societies. It could be stated, arguendo, that the exploitation of the African nations nowadays done by the Africans is a kind of monkey-see-monkey-do type of behaviour copied from the colonial epoch. The people had wrongly learned that national treasures are 'personal possessions' existing mainly for the selfish interests of the person or body of persons who happens to be in charge at any given time period. Their perception is, if it is a national treasure, it is a free-for-all goods that can be used to enrich oneself. The only difference here is that while the colonial master used the proceeds to enrich his 'mother' country, in contemporary Africa, the proceeds are not only channelled to the same old mother country, but this time for the personal interest of the individuals).

Also, "the introduction of regular wages, and their payment to individuals instead of families, is another economic arrangement whose effect on the traditional society has been fundamental. It has given the individual a sense of private power. The levying of taxes on his head which were paid by him, his personal accountability for debts which he incurred and his personal expiation, under the metropolitan jurisdiction, of all the crimes which he committed, the conversion of individuals instead of families to Christianity, with the Christian New Testament, but not Old Testament teaching, of the exclusive accountability of the individual conscience to God, together increased his sense of atomism. He was thus encouraged to think and act more on an atomistic, and less on a communalistic, basis."[15]

The foregoing citation is a double edged sword which must be wielded with caution. It is almost nauseating to blame almost all the social ills in contemporary Africa on the legacy of European influence. Although there is some element of truth concerning European atomistic system of life displacing the African communalistic type, European influence cannot be said to be the creator of selfishness in Africa. All the European influence did was to bolster the existing elements of individualism.

Furthermore, it could be argued that Africans of old and new should be ethically and morally accountable for their deeds and misdeeds. Besides, there have been some elements of the sense of atomism existing in Africa either before or at the arrival of the Europeans.

The colonialists therefore, are not solely culpable in this theory of atomism and its effect with regards to self-aggrandizement. African chiefs and kings of old are equally worthy of blame. Before 1888, the Sultan of Zanzibar, Kenya, acquiesced a large Kenyan territory and its administration to Sir W. Mackinnon who, with other businessmen later went into the interior to ask the chiefs to give away more lands for a token of gifts. In Ghana, when the Europeans arrived, they gave enticements of money and goods to the chiefs many of whom signed away concessions and acquiesced parcels of land which by custom and tradition, they did not have the right to sell. This way the African chiefs and kings gave away their birth-rights for a token pot of pottage. They gave away that which belonged, not to them individually but, to the community at large.

Why would they do that? *Nemo dat quod non habet* (no one gives out what he does not have). Should we give out what we don't have or own, the world would go back to its original state of existence - void and without form. Everything, de facto, would be given away.

Either it is in their blood, or they have failed to learn from the blunder of their forefathers. Contemporary Africans still give away their national treasures for mere tokens. A Sierra Leone administrator who sold a large chunk of diamonds worth billions of dollars for only under ten million, is a case in point. With such in mind, it would be easy to understand that if everyone inclines to siphon the national treasures of their respective nations, no nation could maintain its statehood; nor could economic developments ever be attained. As did concerning the slave trade, an argument can be made at this juncture: if the Africans are willing to sell their national treasures, shouldn't the metropolitans be inclined to buy? Who should be blamed; the Africans who are selling, or the metropolitans who are buying? Are such follies not indicative of inferiority complex?

Whatever answer you may come up with, it could be arguably stated that Africans are still suffering from the ills of political and social humiliation handed down to them by the colonialist. For one thing, Africans still lack self-confidence in themselves. For another thing, they are still myopic in appreciating the worth of their natural resources.

Yet for another, they learned not to have confidence in their own national products. Even though they are capable of producing quality goods, Africans "became reliant upon the outside world, and more particularly upon the United Kingdom, for practically everything we used in our daily life."[16] Although the raw materials were drawn from Africa, they were processed in Europe. The finished products were brought back to Africa and sold to the people at cut-throat prices.

Three reasons could account for why the colonialist preferred to process the material products in Europe: first, to hinder the Africans from learning how to process the raw materials gotten from their midst; second, to instil an inferiority complex in the people making them believe that they could not make the products or that the ones made in Europe were better. And the third was, mercantilism: the European businessmen were buying the raw materials at dirt-cheap prices from Africa, and transporting same to their European base; not only because that was where they had their factories, but also because they made fabulous gains from such a transaction.

Be that as it may, an inferiority complex was infused in the African. Such a negative complex has taken a pathetic toll on the people. Till today, a Nigerian, Ghanaian, or Ivorian would prefer products made in England, France, Italy, or Germany to the ones made in his home country -considering the products made in Europe to be superior to those made by the black man. Inferiority complex therefore, has unknowingly, enveloped the Africans making them believe that anything white is better than anything black -ranging from the white man to his country to his ideas to his products. In Igbo-land of Nigeria for example, the people are very ingenious in industry and very shrewd in manufacturing and technology. However, it is not uncommon to see an Ibo despising an Igbo product, branding it "Igbo-made" with a sarcasm that could send chills down the spines of any indigenous inventor. Such negativism is enough to dampen the spirit of creative inventiveness. Nor is it uncommon to see products made in Nigeria carrying phony labels: "made in England," or "made in Italy," or "made in Japan," etc. It is also not uncommon in that part of the world, Igbo-land, as well as amongst the Yorubas, to see people bragging that they (or their friends and/or relatives have been to or still) are in *obodo-oyibo* or *ala bekee* (the white man's country). When inferiority complex permeates so deep into the peoples of a nation that they are no longer proud of their own creativity, that nation is a long way from recovery. Also, the inferiority complex has a psychological hold on the Africans making them believe the black man is incapable of self-governance. It is up to the Africans to either submerge themselves in this colonial myth and drown in it, or to swim to the reality that the black man can rule himself as well as the white man.

The black man has no other choice but to compete with the white man for the leadership and control of the destinies of his own nation. If only the black man could learn and know that only the black man can control the destiny of his own nation. If only he could have confidence in himself. If only he could be proud of his creativity. If only he would stop defrauding his own nation. Then, ours could still become a great continent.

However, this lesson was not learned. And, it is not being learned. What was learned instead was how to satisfy egoistic interests at the expense of others. While the colonial attitude was the winner takes all, the African attitude is the leader (or the rule)takes all.

The African premier politicians learned it from their colonial masters and passed it down to the modern politicians and/or their military counterparts. Take for instance the IBO coinage (I-Before-Others) as well as the policy of one Administrator and the comment he made: *"onye ube lulu nya lachaa"* (i.e. if riches or wealth falls within your spell or disposition, whether it is ill-acquired or not, enjoy it, for it's all yours). This kind of statement and/or attitude deserves serious disdain and repudiation. The author of that philosophy should know that great nations were never born, they were made. If the leaders of the great nations were to have selfishly enjoyed the wealth of their nations because it fell within their administrative spells, there ought not be great nations today.

There is no doubt that the welfare and prosperity of the United States could never have been achieved if its leaders pursued their personal, intrinsic goals. It achieved its prosperity, because its leaders continuously pursue the national interest. For a nation to develop socially, technologically, economically, and politically, its leaders must divest themselves of selfishness, and exorcise their minds of any malpurpose, as pertains to national treasure.

Even some of the administrators who had repudiated colonial rip-offs and those who had gone to Europe and/or other Western nations and seen how things are done differently, toe the same old line of not caring about the collective interest of their nation. They believe that as long as they achieve their personal desires in the process, the end justifies the means.

Such an attitude has been adopted wholesale not only in politics but also in religion and other aspects of the peoples' life. Much like "the pioneer Christian missionaries betrayed a neglect and misunderstanding of the people's way of life, modern evangelizers and/or missionaries toe almost the same line..."[17] Both the colonialists and the missionaries paid little or no regard to the local conditions or needs; so do African politicians and ordinary citizens. All toeing the same path formed by the colonial master; thereby, creating social, economic, and political instability in contemporary Africa. That legacy of the colonial system still thrives in modern Africa.

The people have, hitherto, not found a system that works for them. They still toe the path left behind by the colonialists. First, when the missionaries came in, they did not pay attention to the people's culture and existing way of life - the socio-politics. When their colonial brothers came in, they did not give a hoot either. Then when the newly emerged African politicians took over from the colonial master, they were more interested in self-governance than they were in paying attention to the minute details of how the system works. Nor were the colonialists interested in coaching them, other than fleeing with their spoils. They came. They saw. They took. Whatever was happening next to the political and economic development of the nations they defrauded, they did not care about. Unfortunately, this happens to be the same attitude and mentality adopted by most contemporary Third World politicians, ranging from Latin America to Asia to Africa. Whatever is happening to the economy of their respective nations, they do not care much about. To such people, personal interest overrides national interest.

It is still mind boggling and/or perplexing to me as to why those that choose to fleece their nations decide to deposit their spoils overseas. Is it the case of amassing wealth in a safe haven where "bugs" and "termites" could not tamper with it? If this is the reason, it is rippled with idiocy. What happens to that treasure, if the host country decides to nationalize all foreign assets? Who loses and who gains from the adventure of transferring national treasure overseas? It is understandable, though not pardonable, that the colonial master transferred resources from the colonies to his home-base. Should the person of colour follow in the same footsteps – to debase the economy of his own nation? Isn't it foolhardy to do so? As far as I am concerned, an adjective has not yet been coined nor can any be found in any language with which to qualify the person or group of persons who subjects himself to the position of relegating the economy of his home-state to the precarious status-quo. Thus, whosoever defrauds his nation and/or debases the economy thereof, it should be better for him to be cast into the lagoon, with a millstone tied around his neck: for he who is not concerned with the economic solidarity and political development of his nation, is not worthy to live.

A going beyond or a transcendence of the old colonial mentality is still at work in our midst. As the modern evangelizers toe the lines of the colonial missionaries, in like manner, the contemporary African politicians toe almost the, same line as did their colonial masters - taking, and taking, and taking. In the same vein, following the same exact footprint of his former master, takes the spoils to the same place as did the colonialist (to the metropolitan banks in metropolitan countries); all to the detriment of his own nation. For instance, the *El Comercio* of the first week of February 1997 revealed that the Ecuadorian president, Abdala Bucaram, had about seventeen million dollars in his foreign bank-account. And, before his death, "the half-billion in his bank-account... made Nkrumah by all odds the world's richest African nationalist..."[18]

Also, the International Herald Tribune of Friday February 2, 1990 cited Nigeria's Babangida as the Third World's richest leader (ruler). Late General Sani Abacha later topped Babangida as the most corrupt and the richest leader (or actually ruler) in Third World countries. Several years after his death, the several billions of dollars he hid in various countries around the world are yet to be recovered. In Nigeria, even State Governors are not innocent of corruption. For example, according to Nigeria's Newsdigest, as much as $163 million was traced to Abubakar Atiku Bugudu, the governor of Kebbi State, in Nigeria. The puzzle, however, is that the Nigerian government (in Muhammadu Buhari's administration) makes no effort to recover such a loot, especially if the looter happens to be a Muslim, or belongs in the same political party as Buhari). The news caption below explains more.

Should one join hands to continue where the colonizer stopped, nothing would be left for the children and the posterity of that continent. A kingdom that debases its own economy cannot develop. The idea of stopping misappropriation of funds had, purportedly, been the centripetal element of military intervention in politics. This is so because, whenever such a misappropriation happens, or is perceived to be happening, the military comes in and ruffles the feathers of the existing order. Such a nation thus falls back to square one. Like a cracked record, the same song repeats itself – over, and over, and over - and perhaps will happen so, world without end.

To break the circle, serious minded politicians should pay more attention to the national interest rather than personal ones. For in achieving national goals, personal ones are also achieved. National goals can never be achieved by pursuing selfish ends – it has to be the other way around. Altruistic tendencies should be the norm. Thus: seek ye first the national interest and everything else will be added unto you.

Had this been the credo of our politicians, ours could have become strong nations –economically and politically, to say the least. Either there were not enough educated elite to assist the premier politicians in maintaining focus toward actualizing the national political goal – political and economic emancipation, or they cared more about political and less about economic –failing to realize that none can augur well without the other.

Or, perhaps they were more interested in filling their speeches with rodomontade than in seeking solutions to replenish that which had been stolen from their nations. Or, were they interested in amassing their own fortune?

It would be fallacious to entirely blame the premier politicians for their failure to maintain political developments in the 'new' nations. One should recall that most of the African nations won their independence in late 1950s and early 1960s. Military interference started taking place by the mid 1960s. Several reasons account for that. First, it has been noted above that the colonizers were not interested in teaching their ex-colonies the rudiments of Western political systems. It could be clearly stated that, perhaps, if the ex-colonies were taught the elements of the political system being handed to them, there would not have been socio-political disturbances soon after independence was won. The turbulence that ensued in most of the new nations soon after self-rule was gotten, stifled the confidence that black man can rule himself by any peaceful means. This should not be so. If Nelson Mandela could rule South Africa, black man is capable of effective governance. The major reason for the failure of democracy in post-independence Africa is that the nationalists did not learn the rudiments of the system well enough.

The colonizers stayed in those colonies for more than one hundred years, from 1800s to the 1950s and 60s. For example, the British acquisition of Nigeria started in 1861 when Lagos was annexed as a colony. Nigeria won its independence in late 1960. Within this nearly one hundred years of occupation the colonialist could have taught the principles of the Western political system to the people if they had the inclination to do so.

Besides, it would be an error filled with misunderstanding and falsity to blame the fathers of African Nationalism for their rush toward independence without waiting any further to learn any more than they already did. Had they waited any longer, the exploitation could have, like wildfire, conflagrated into new areas unbeknownst to the nationalists, thus they inclined to achieve self-governance with greater promptitude than more dialectics. They had understood the concept of colonialism, that it was tantamount to political enslavement and economic thralldom.

Another factor worthy of examination is the land where the system fell. It could be succinctly argued that the Western political system was cultivated in an infertile soil not meant for it. This may have precipitated a great deal of political instability. This fact was even recognized by some colonial administrators such as Lord Lugard who finally realized "that the imposition of foreign institutions upon an alien culture could hardly hope to succeed. Moreover, Lord Hailey argued, 'We have hitherto followed the model of our own parliamentary institutions but it. Is by no means certain that we have here the part of government best suited to colonial conditions. After 1960, the truth of Lord Hailey's words became apparent... the so-called Westminster model of government" did not work, and has not worked ever since, at least, for the most part.[19] Another "obvious example is that in a state with a strongly differentiated tribal substructure the effectiveness of the authority of the central government and the nature of the subject's loyalty to it will be of different order from that which is normal in non-tribal Western societies."[20] Thus while the Western system works for the Westerners, it has problems germinating on African soil. And things have consistently gone awry ever since its inception.

Whatever the case may be, Western political idiosyncrasy is now the only known system of civil polity. The people should have to study the system and make it work in their nations irrespective of tribal and social differences. This may not be as much out of choice as it should be of necessity. Should one argue from now till thy kingdom come, it is obvious that nothing brings socio-economic developments in a nation more than a stable political environment. And that can only be achieved by reaching consensus on what stable system of government to adopt.

In conclusion, Africa and its people have changed a great deal since the metropolitan influence which stretched five hundred years back. The impact became more profound from 1885 till this day and, perhaps, will continue to be so for ever andever, unless something is done to forestall it. The majority of Africans have, heretofore, pursued their new-found metropolitan idiosyncrasies to the utter neglect of their culture and tradition. The African fervently follows the metropolitan ideas in anything and everything be it in social, in political, in religious, or in economic arenae.

More so with the first three, than the fourth one which, indeed, should have been the one to copy the most. Because the economic area is in serious neglect, disaster has been the case, spilling over to other socio-political fabrics of our nations. In the sphere of religion, I intended to set the record straight with regard to our forefathers and their religious beliefs. They were not Devil worshippers, as they were falsely accused. They worshipped the Almighty God. I did not say people did not worship the Devil. If they did, the number must have been very insignificant. As a matter of fact, there are still many Satanists (or devil worshippers) in the metropolitan countries, including the United States of America, Canada and Europe.

In the same vein, I am not alluding to the existence or nonexistence of magic for that is a mystery beyond my comprehension. If it existed, it existed, and still does exist, everywhere including Europe. However, that of the African has always been condemned and repressed as something evil, whilst that of the West receives little, or no, criticisms.

Nevertheless, this is not a platform, nor is it a conference-table to debate which is wrong and which is right. And, "I do not propose to stir up a hornet's nest by making a generalization that African magic is pseudo-scientific, but I submit that continuous belief in the same is having a deleterious effect on African mentality.

I exist in the world, yet I believe that the same world is infested by beings which are destructive in their mission. This kind of thinking leads one to believe that a wicked man with "medicine" can dispose of a kindly man who has no "medicine" to stand the challenge of his detractors."[21] True though this may be, the totality of African Traditional religious belief was not bad, at least, it was not what the early missionaries purported it to be. We should not be zombies. We should always examine what we are imbibing ourselves in. And for those in our midst who regard others as Devils at worst or enemies at best, it should serve as a memento when we look at another being, to treat them with respect upon remembering that our freedom of religion ends where another's begins. If a person or group of persons accepts your beliefs, so be it. If not, leave the people to their system and you are welcome to yours. No matter what we believe in, we should not destroy our ancestral memorabilia. It belongs to our ancestors, not to us. I advise we pay more attention to the economy for now; religious and other matters will take care of themselves subsequently.

CHAPTER THREE

Neo-Colonialism

Here comes the con man
Coming with his con plan
We won't take no bribes
We've got to stay alive
We gonna chase those crazy bald heads
out of our town.[22]

-Bob Marley

Direct colonization has come and gone. But its effect still remains. The effect has not only been planted in African soil but in African mind, in African soul, and in African blood. The imperialists now use the Africans to debilitate their nation's economy by indirect means - neo-colonialism.

Neo-colonialism was the new system of exploitation devised by the colonialist either before or soon after political independence had been granted to the colonized nations. It could be seen as a disguised form of imperialism. Its vehicle of operation was fragmentation which in itself, was an extension of the 'divide-and-rule' policy. While colonialism entailed direct rule over the colonies, neo-colonialism maintained control of the colonies (or ex-colonies) by indirect approach. Neo-colonialism, therefore, could be defined as a system of domination setup by the colonialist, using indirect political approach to maintain a hegemony over the cultural and economic destinies of a nation.

According to Nnamdi Azikiwe, the relationship existing between Africa and the British Empire is still evolutional. Equally, Chinua Achebe, observed in his novel that, 'the West has not put the final touches to creation, it is morning yet on creation day.[1]

The metropolitan West has always found one method of exploitation to replace the other within the African continent in particular and the Third World nations in general. A close observation of the relationship maintained by the metropolitan west with the African continent has not failed to reveal one systematic exploitation or another; first Slave-trade, then Direct colonization, now Indirect hegemony or Nee-colonialism, Nkwame Nkrumah refers to neo-colonialism as balkanization which he used, "to describe the breaking up of Africa into small, weak states, since it arose from the action of the great powers when they divided up the European part of the old Turkish Empire, and created a number of dependent and competing states in the Balkan Peninsula."[23]

Whatever name, shape, or form it takes, the principle of neo-colonialism is essentially the same. The United States' presence in the Philippines by way of military-bases could be seen as a form of neo-colonialism. And so is its presence in Latin Africa through indirect administrative policy. The United States maintains its holdings in these areas largely for its security interests, political interests (imperialism) and economic interests (exploitation). Imperialism can be defined as: aggressive political process used by one nation to maintain hegemony over the political and, sometimes, economic developments of another nation. For example, the United States intervention in the Cuban/Spanish war, its acquisition of the Panama canal-zone, and its intervention in Nicaragua (in 1912), and Dominican Republic in 1916, happened only for imperialistic and exploitative reasons. As a matter of fact, much like other imperialists, the United States was the major obstacle to economic, social, and political development in Latin America. This has, on occasion, prompted anti-US sentiments within the region one of which was the widespread rioting directed at then vice-president Richard Nixon during his tour of major South American states; another was the Cuban revolution of 1959.

Also, in quest of maintaining political and economic control over the region, John F. Kennedy's administration provided arms for the assassination of Trujillo of the Dominican Republic in 1961. The United States' presence in the US Virgin Islands in the West Indies could also be seen as a good example of neo-colonialism. One should not make the mistake of accusing only the West of imperialism. Not long ago, the East (Soviet Union) decided to toe the colonialist path as the West did, and has made its own impact on East Africa. Nor should one forget the influence the Arab world has had, particularly on North Africa, and other countries of Africa wherein some have adopted Arabic names, or in some cases where a nation transformed itself into Arab Republic, for example, Somalia. Of course, even the Dutch were involved, for they had taken and occupied South Africa.

In whatever shape or form imperialism comes, the end result is always the same -exploitation. Whether it was perpetrated by the Arabs, or the United States, or Europe or Russia, the policy is the same and the end result is equally the same; whether it was done to the Latinos, or to Asians, or to the Africans. The most obvious ways of entrapment are through IMF high-interest-loans and devaluation of the nation's local currency (bringing the value to next to nothing). A case in point is Nigeria which, in spite of its oil boom, is experiencing ever-increasing economic woes since after the devaluation of its currency. Ghana and most other African nations have had similar experiences. It makes me wonder, do the African leaders ever learn lessons from each other's plights. Did they have to personally experience it, in order to realize that, a snake which swallowed the mouse will also swallow the lizard, if caution is not taken? Third World leaders ought to have known that the First World countries would prefer, and will always find the means, to keep them in Third World condition. If one has not yet realized it from the episodes of the past five-hundred years then 'am afraid, one will never realize it. It does not take a genius to figure out that "however much money a Third World country may have, it is a hidden purpose of IMF strategy to fleece and bankrupt it, and hand the proceeds over to Western creditors for debt trap peonage, A succinct description of debt trap peonage is supplied by Cheryl Payer in the following passage from his book The Debt Trap (1974):

The system can be compared point by point with peonage on an individual scale. In the peonage, or debt slavery system, the worker is unable to use his nominal freedom to leave the service of his employer, because the latter supplies him with credit (for overpriced goods in the company store) necessary to supplement his meagre wages. The aim of the employer creditor/ merchant is neither to collect the debt once and for all, nor to starve the employee to death, but rather to keep the labourer permanently indentured through his debt to the employer. The worker cannot run away, for other employers and the state recognize the legality of his debt; nor has he any hope of earning his freedom with his low wages, which do not keep pace with what he consumes, let alone the true value of what he produces for his master. Precisely the same system operates on the international level. Nominally independent countries find that their debts, and their constant inability to finance current needs out of exports, keep them tied by a tight leash to their creditors. The IMF orders them, in effect, to continue laboring on the plantation, while it refuses to finance their efforts to get up in business for themselves... this is debt slavery on an international scale. If they remain within the system, the debtor countries are doomed to perpetual underdevelopment, or rather to development of their exports at the service of multinational enterprises, at the expense of development for the needs of their own citizens"[24]

When Jesus said: to those who have, more are given. And those who have not, even the little they have is taken away from them and given to those who already have, so they could have even more abundantly; I do not think He had the IMF in mind when He said that. Neither did He recruit anyone or any institution to be a disciple through which such prophesy could be fulfilled. Nor did one expect the IMF (or any other neo-colonialist interest) to be the instrument through which Third World nations are relegated to economic squalor; or appended to high interest loans with monumental repercussions. Nevertheless, though such is neo-colonialism in the first degree, no one forced the victimnations into such predicaments. Their leaders did. Thus, although one points an accusing finger at the metropolitan powers, the Third World leaders are much more culpable.

Be that as it may, in most cases, the process covertly starts when the metropolitan "power forces the conclusion of pacts with the balkanized states which give control of their foreign policy to the former". Thus, the neo-colonized states inadvertently sign away their rights; thereafter, their independence exists only in name, "for their liberty ...is gone."[25]

With the exception of Ghana, must African nations became fragmented into Regions, immediately after their attainment of independence. For example, Nigeria was divided into three regions. Ruanda-Urundi was also divided up at independence. Following Nkrumah's philosophy, one may be tempted to postulate that the motive behind this was to weaken the cohesiveness of the people much further. But one must bear in mind that there wasn't much cohesiveness amongst the people before the advent of colonialism. If anything, colonialism, by means of conventional education, cemented most of, if not all, the inter-tribal warfare. Through the sagacious understanding which such education may have bestowed on them, the people have, for the most part, found it at least reticent to engage in such inter-tribal scuffles.

In Nkrumah's perspective, Africa was balkanized or divided up into small and antagonistic regions. Nkrumah's theory that balkanization is synonymous with neo-colonialism is some-what debatable. If his theory of balkanization alludes to scramble and partition of Africa by metropolitan powers, he scores a point in that. If, however, his yard stick of measuring balkanization was drawn from the notion that the new African nations were regionalized with ulterior motives (on the metropolitan part) to draw the individual small states into antagonistic skirmishes, then his theory is lacking substance. If mistrust and squabbles eventually crept in between the peoples of one region and another, though it could be said to be as a result of territorial regionalization, it could not be said that such was the original motive for which the regions were created.

Nevertheless, Nkrumah's allegation cannot be thrown away without closer scrutiny. He sees balkanization as the instrument of neo-colonialism; and balkanization gives birth to mistrust which in turn brings about regional conflicts. While it could be argued that ethnic conflicts were in existence in Africa before the advent of the metropolitan administration, regionalization did not exorcise the spirit of mistrust from amongst the people; for instance, the Yorubas, Igbos, Hausas, Ibibios, Efiks, Tivs, and other ethnic groups of Nigeria do not have much trust, if any, for each other. Regionalization did not make it any better; if anything, it made it worse, as people would have the tendency to bond more with their individual states. Yakubu Gowon learned this from his British mentors; and his successor, Murtala Muhammed, used it to weaken the unity of the Igbos, after the civil war. The Ibos used to be close-knit when in one state – East Central State. But when they became Split in two - Anambra, and Imo states, some elements of disunity crept in between the two. Things have even gone more awry, as these two states have gotten further fragmentation, as did other states in Nigeria.

Mistrust and internal rivalries happen as much in Nigeria as in any other ex-colony. For instance, after Guyana attained its independence in 1964, "the issue was no longer just the Guyanese versus the British. It was one set of Guyanese against another set of Guyanese. Likewise, it was one set of Trinidadians against another set.

And in Jamaica...it was...a question of the progressive elements as opposed to the more conservative elements in the society."[26] The foregoing, basically, verifies Nkrumah's contention that balkanization breeds antagonism, and is an instrument of colonialism.

However, metropolitan administrators were not always pro-fragmentation. There were instances of amalgamation of one region and another as opposed to fragmentation. A case in point was the 1914 amalgamation of Northern and Southern Nigeria. In some other instances, the metropolitan administrators were known to have attempted to ameliorate disputes and bring in tranquillity within the colonies, as evidenced also in Nigeria, when in 1953 there was a feud in Kano, which burst into ugly flame of violence.

Serious riots broke out as the Northern emirs refused to allow the Southern (Yoruba-based) Action Group Party to hold a public rally. Rioting occurred for three-long days; and 46 people were killed while more than 200 others were injured. Martial law was passed. "As the Manchester Guardian put it; "One thing is quite clear. This is a clash of Nigerians against Nigerians, not against the British." On May 21, a few days after the riots, the British Colonial Secretary announced that the constitution would have to be amended 'to provide for greater Regional autonomy and for removal of powers of intervention by the Center in matters which could without detriment to other Regions, be placed entirely within Regional competence.' Conferences were held in both London and Lagos on the issue of amending the constitution. Tempers ran high and objectives seemed irreconcilable among the Nigerians, but finally agreement was obtained for a new system, called the federation of Nigeria, which gave precise guarantees to the various regions against encroachment from the federal government.

For the first time, the powers of government were divided between the regions and thecenter."[27] Through this medium, the colonialist sought to bring peace rather than rancor in a troubled region. Great Britain, perhaps, may have settled the squabbles because it had a vestige interest in the region. Their amelioration of the strife in that area, does not by any indication mean that they cared more for the welfare of that region than they cared about maintaining its synthesis for their continual exploitation.

Whatever form it takes, neo-colonialism is a mirror-image (or another face) of colonialism. Thus, whether it is called direct or indirect colonialism, old or new colonialism, or christened neo-colonialism, it is still the same colonialism. The only thing that changed is the method of operation. It could even come with a different name called "Protectorate," whereby, the metropolitan power signs a pact with the subject country, to "protect" the latter against any aggression from any other metropolitan power.

This, though, was on a quid-pro-quo basis. The subject country, would have some obligation to render to the power which "protects" it. The relationship between Puerto Rico and the United States could be seen in this light. In Nigeria, both the Oil River areas and Lagos, became British Protectorates in 1885 and 1888 respectively. In 1890, Uganda became a British Protectorate. Kenya became a British Protectorate in 1895.

Thenceforth, these nations became British subjects, just for minimal protection from Britain. This, of course, paved the way for Complete and direct colonization. The difference between colonialism and neo-colonialism is that the former used direct means while the other uses Indirect Approach. For instance, in Latin America, not only did Spain and Portugal directly extract the mineral wealth from the American colonies, they directly, humiliatingly subjected the Native Americans to slave labor.

The colonialists and some theologians firmly believed that the Native Americans were by nature inferior to Europeans. Based on this assumption, the Native American Indians were directly forced in one way or another to work for the colonialists. Sometimes they were distributed among the Spanish settlers in a system called*encomienda*.

According to this system, the people were to work for the colonialists and to supply a tribute in goods or cash, in return for minimal protection and for "being taught Christianity and the Spanish way of life."[28]

The colonizing powers greedily grabbed the natural riches of Latin America as much as was the case in Africa and other colonized Third World nations. Thus, colonialism vis-à-vis exploitation became a process that had the result, among others, of leaving the colonies considerably poorer than they otherwise would have been after independence.

Yet, after the colonies had won their independence, this new system was devised to still maintain authority over the nations' cultural, economic and political conditions, albeit, by remote or indirect means: Neo-colonialism.

In Nkrumah's point of view, neo-colonialism "creates client states, independent in name but in point of fact pawns of the very colonial power which is supposed to have given them independence."[29] Nkrumah knew what he was talking about when he used the phrase pawns. During his regime, "a reserve of about $550 million derived from the pre-independence cocoa boom was transformed into a massive international debt amounting to at least half that figure."[30] This, subsequently, resulted in continuous budget deficits which eventually culminated in inflation and more austerity budgets. The European neo-colonialists found it necessary to maintain a quid pro quo relationship with the ex-colonies, as they needed raw materials for their industries, and market for the finished products. The relationship could not be said to be a parallel quid pro quo; the neo-colonialist gains more from the relationship than client-state does. As a matter of fact, it drains the client-state more than it replenishes – just like giving a rabbit a carrot with one hand while holding a stick in the other.

Much so, when aids in loans are given to the client-states, they are given enough rope to hang themselves. Although this can be argued to be one of the reasons the Third World nations are perpetually in debt, the main reasons the Third World nations wallow in poverty are within, not without, the nations. In this modern age and time, in my opinion, a majority of the economic and political woes can be blamed on maladministration and/or mismanagement of policy and misappropriation of funds, in the respective countries. The rest can be blamed on the treat-or-trick of neo-colonialism. It is one thing for a country to receive billions of dollars in loans, it is another thing for the funds to be used effectively in actualizing a meaningful purpose.

Anything contrary to this, is not only self-defeating but drags the nation(s) into a snow ball of debt; and entraps the nation(s) in a vicious-circle-of-poverty. Nigeria is a case in point. The economic hardship she is now facing was self-inflicted. Nigeria was not forced into this situation. Rather, she volunteered herself into it. In 1978, when she borrowed the first billion, she had far more revenue from oil than she could sensibly spend. In spite of the fact that she did not need the money, Nigeria still got herself into borrowing. This was expressed by Olusegun Obasanjo. In his own words he mentioned that: "In 1977 and 1978, at the time of slight dip in the oil market, international bankers were descending upon my government in droves. They pressed the case that our economic strength was such that we were grossly under borrowed, especially for a nation with such a visionary development program...that led to our first jumbo loan of $20 billion. Unfortunately, our successors in government succumbed more readily to the bankers' siren song which led to...debt of some $20 billion, assuring us membership in the distinguished club of insolvent Third World countries."[31]

It was therefore evident that after her first taste of borrowing, Nigeria went adrift into more and more borrowing of billions and billions of dollars. Yet, she was borrowing what she never needed. According to the World Bank's record, in 1987, Nigeria's outstanding debt had gotten to $27.0 billion, and the debt service amount, from 1987 to 1989, was 12.2 billion. The foregoing does not include the interests which could be more than $5 billion per year; thus, entrapping the citizens and their posterity in debt.

Simple arithmetic reveals that the principal amount compounds with the interest amount to give birth to more interests, and so on, and so forth. Does it make sense?

> O, Mighty nation,
> Where are the wits
> Of thy children?

Nigeria, with all her educated elite and academicians – Lawyers, Mathematicians, Economists, Financial management administrators, Bankers, Statisticians, Accountant, Advisors, Analysts, Educators, Political Scientists, and what have you, should have been able to know the implication of entrapping the nation in debt. Perhaps to them the saying: A borrower is a sorrower, only exists in The Student's Companion. Even Adam Smith and Richardo (in the ancient times), knew the economic repercussions of such debt and the force with which it debases the wealth of a nation. "According to a report in the Broad Street Journal of December 1983, the permanent secretary in the Ministry of Finance, Mr. Abubakar Alhaji, tried... to gain the support of the Nigerian Labor Congress for the government's efforts to get an IMF loan. He explained to them that the most crucial benefit Nigeria needs from the IMF loan was the restoring of international confidence in Nigeria, a confidence which would enable Nigeria to secure additional loans from the capital market."[32] Common sense teaches us that the only thing that can restore confidence and dignity on (a person or) a nation (as the case may be), is not going into debt, but staying out of it. It does not take a genius to know that debt does not restore confidence. It rather creates rancor and/ or sorrow; be it in a person or a nation.

It creates restlessness, and reduces the debtor-nation from free-nation to financial and economic-slavery, appended by debt, to the financial and economic welfare of the creditor-nation. Whereby, the debtor (nation and its citizens) will live the rest of their lives in such a bondage, living in penury and struggling to pay debts. In the same vein, such is the incubus Mexico, Venezuela, Argentina, Morocco, and the Philippines have to grapple with. A look at the current World Bank's Global Development Finance, which replaced the World Debt Tables (please go to the Internet: World Wide Web at "WWW.World Bank. ORG/WDI/" enter. Obtain a copy and see for yourself; as this), will reveal that most of these countries' debts have since doubled, tripled, or even quadrupled from that seen at the end of this Chapter. By-and-large, these countries' debt-entrapments could have been avoided had they used their brains and their resources to their own advantage.

But, assuming one became a numskull and therefore incapable of using one's brain to know the implication of entrapping oneself in debt, one should have taken a deep and starry look at the predicament facing Brazil as it toils and wallows in its debt of more than $100 billion. It would be a nightmare should Nigeria or any other Third World nation face the same or similar predicament.

At the end of May, 1996, US newspapers like the Democrat & Chronicle, and the Times Union of Rochester, New York, listed Nigeria as the number-one nation in the world infested with crime and corruption (in a list of ten, which included Russia and Brazil, among others).

In the direction Nigeria is drifting, if she does not pay off her debt (the sooner, the better) and stay debt-free, her situation will climax, and may become worse than that of Brazil, considering Nigeria's population of over 100 million. "Now that it has happened and the Western money lenders have their hands on Nigeria's oil revenues, you can expect them to run it down with interest and other charges, till a bankrupt Nigeria will have to do whatever its foreign creditors say it must do."[33] To some extent, a similar scenario replicated itself in General Joseph Mobutu's Zaire, when the nation's mineral resources were mortgaged over to China on account of a loan.

A question now arises: What can be done, to turn most Third World nations around, and prevent them from Brazilian scenario? The only smart answer to this can be repeated a million times: Stop borrowing. Pay off the loans no matter what it takes. Be debt-free. And stay debt-free. If there was any need to borrow, there is nothing wrong with that. But borrowing just for the sake of borrowing, is nothing short of folly. And it is even more so, when the money is not put to effective use (such as economic development and industrialization, etc.), but merely squandered in an unaccountable manner. It is one thing to borrow money, it is yet another thing to utilize it in an efficacious way to produce revenue and the means of repaying the loan. Common sense should teach one that, there is no free lunch; loans come with heavy interest payments besides the principal. And loans don't get washed away. A nation is imprisoned/ entrapped with it. If there was no need for borrowing, it should not be done-period. Debt plummets a nation into social destitution and economic insolvency. Thus, African nations in particular and Third World nations in general should be wise not to allow such fate to befall them. Not to over emphasize it, however, they should study the case of Brazil and learn a lesson from it. Here is its synopsis:

In the 1970s, Brazil went on borrowing spree. Today, its debt is almost $100 billion. Its debt trap agonies fill the headlines these days. Since its exports cannot pay the debt service charges, Brazil is in the treadmill of ...rescheduling ... its debts. But before banks agree to roll over its loans, Brazil has to agree to the austerity measures decreed by the IMF. These measures, however, call for severe hardships to be imposed on the population.

As a result, Brazil has been plunged into semi-permanent social unrest. Strikes, riots, and factory closures have become the disorders of the day. Hunger roams the streets and countryside ... numerous supermarkets were looted by hungry city dwellers. Starving rural folk who fled to the cities were reduced to cannibalism. Indeed, where in the 1970s Brazil went a-borrowing, in the 1980s it has gone a-sorrowing.[34]

The worst mistake a nation could make is to pass the buck, and get into the merry-go-round of debt rescheduling; in which case the debt is never paid off but is prolonged to last from generation to generation, and its interest compounds even more.

Thus, the circle of poverty it creates is endless. Which person, or body of persons, in their right minds would put their nation and its citizens in such a dread? A second question is, if things could go that awry in a nation as small as Brazil, within ten years and with $100 billion in debt,

a) What happened to that money within 10 years?

b) Is debt trap peonage not the reason Mexico remains so poor while its neighbor, the United States, is so affluent?

c) How much worse could things go in such a populous country as Nigeria, if it climbs more into, and buries itself in debt?

Whatever answer you may come up with, the only possible way to break from such a degenerative circle is: stop borrowing, pay off what was borrowed, and save your nations from the abyss of political darkness and economic squalor. More importantly, use the borrowed funds in providing efficient and effective indigenous industries which would not only generate money to pay the debts, but will strengthen the economy of the nations(s), in the long run, thereby, uplifting such nations from Third World to Second, if not First World, level.

The smartest move however, is to denounce greed and not get involved in the first place. The advice of such a political philosopher as William Edward Burghart Du Bois could save our nations from unnecessary self-enslavement. He said:

> Here then my brothers, you face your great decision: will you for temporary advantage for automobiles, refrigerators and Paris gowns - spend your income in paying interest on borrowed funds, or will you sacrifice present comfort and the chance to shine before your neighbours in order to educate your children, develop such industry as best serves the great mass of people and makes your country strong in ability, self-support and self-defence?

Such union of effort for strength calls for sacrifice and self-denial, while the capital offered you at high price by the colonial powers like France, Britain, Holland, Belgium, and the United States, will prolong fatal colonial imperialism, from which you have suffered slavery, serfdom and colonialism.[35]

The restoration of national pride could be achieved through self-confidence (or self- esteem) which ought to start from the leaders downward to the grassroots-level. But some Africans desirous of immediate gratification, as opposed to delayed and gradual actualization of their dreams, opt to grab what they can, while they can; even if that means plunging their nations into economic bondage.

Thus, the pursuit of taste, fashion and/or the new way of life amongst the peoples of the impoverished nations are partly to blame, at least minutely, for the bad state of affairs in social, political and economic spheres.

Balkanization or partition, though quite influential on the African continent, "partition without Europeanisation might not have changed Africa profoundly... The enormousness of the change they induced might be judged by estimating how much a young African adult of 1984 would have in common with his great-great-grandfather, who was probably a young man in 1884. In their languages, dress, homes, modes of transport, and distances they could travel; in their beliefs,

Social ideals, marriage rites, and even the foods they ate, the two would be very different.

"In all likelihood, the young African of 1984 would have more in common with the European of 1984 than with his own great-great-grandfather. "One not-so-obvious area in which this century-long cultural shift is afflicting Africa in 1984 is its inability to feed its population. We may be reasonably sure that Africa did not import food in 1884... But today, a century later, Africa is plagued by hunger and appeals by African governments for more and more food aid have become routine."[36] Thus, Africa's economic woes could be blamed on metropolitan influence.

All in all, the questions that need be asked are: what now should be done to abate the situation? If in 1884 Africans were autarkic, but merely a hundred years later (by 1984), the continent plummeted into hunger and starvation, what will be its fate in another one hundred years, if nothing is done to reverse the trend?

"Of course, desertification, drought and wars...account for some of the need...' However, 'with European-style education and the enormous prestige and rewards of bureaucratic work, millions of Africans...drifted from farming to various kinds of clerking. This massive shift from production to administration has weakened the farm base of Africa."[37] This is perhaps the root of the problem of hunger and starvation that now plague Africa.

In this regard the people are to blame for their myopic mind, stymied sight, and ineptness. It is time one realized that neither academics nor anything else augurs well in an empty stomach. Much like was discussed in chapter two, the major problems which created the sufferings in contemporary Africa emanate from misplaced priorities and the tendency to, wrongfully, assume that we know it all. And thus, the propensity to disdain the ancient wisdom of our forefathers, which worked well for them and, instead, toe the path of the metropolitans.

It is a paradox that the Westerners, whose lifestyle we copy, do very well in their own nations, economy-wise. Without heeding the repercussion, perhaps not even realizing it, most Africans tend to hinge only on the ephemeral benefits of Western education rather than use it on a broader scope to achieve a deep-rooted, long-lasting, result beneficial to all and sundry. For example, in Nigeria, the act of acquiring Western education is more for prestige and social or ethnic superiority of those who have it verses those who don't. The comment of Obafemi Awolowo in 1947, exemplifies this notion. He said:

> "In embracing Western culture, the Yorubas take the lead, and have benefited immensely as a result. The Efiks, the Ijaws, the Ibibios and the Ibos come next...The Hausas, and Fulanis on the other hand are extremely conservative, and take reluctantly to Western civilization..."[38]

Though this assertion is well-founded and was no more true in those days than it is today, one should not fail to realize that while these other tribes have been busy pursuing the Western civilization, the Hausas and the Fulanis have been busy feeding the nation. (For example, meat, poultry, onions, tomatoes, etc., come from Northern Nigeria). On the other hand, the reluctance of the Hausas and Fulanis to embrace Western Education has delayed and hindered Nigeria from moving forward in areas of Science, Industrialization, Computer, and Technology. Worst still, the backwardness emanating from the Hausas and Fulanis is what has given birth to Boko Haram and Fulani herdsmen jihadist terrorists in modern Nigeria.

While there is nothing wrong with the pursuit of Western civilization, it is one thing to pursue it and actualize it; and it is quite another thing to put it to an effective use. For the life of me, I have not yet heard of starvation in the metropolitan west. The Europeans whom the Africans emulate, with all their education, never abandoned farm-work, nor have they displaced it with the 'more-prestigious-bureaucratic/ administrative' work. They (the Europeans) know the quiddity or the inherent nature or the essence or the importance of all social strata, and they maintain each stratum accordingly.

Society would go awry, should one social stratum displace the other without adequate refurbishment. He, who is seeking education, will have to swim or sink with it, after achieving it. I suggest we swim. Education is good; however, it is not pursued just for the sake of pursuing it. When applied well, the acquiring of it is beneficial for effective development of oneself, one's community, one's nation. Also, the acquisition of education subsequently paves the way for peace and harmony amongst us. By and large, it also promotes smooth and peaceful accord in international relations.

This being the case, one can succinctly argue that, the ultimate goal in pursuing education is: Development. In the absence of applying what has been learned toward the development of a nation, what value is a nation full of educated elites, but cannot feed itself? This is the core problem in not only Nigeria, but Africa in general.

What is done with education, after it has been acquired, is the yard-steak with which to measure what has been learned and what impact (negative or positive) it has had either on oneself, community, or nation. If after acquiring it, it creates independence (in all its social, political, and economic ramifications), then it has had a positive effect, judging from the standard mentioned above, in terms of Development.

If, on the other hand, it creates more and more dependency (whether in social, political, or economic areas) of one entity on another (be it person on person, or nation on nation), then one must pause to ask: What is going on here? Why? And what can be done to remedy that which has gone wrong either in self, community, or nation?

In spite of all the educated and intellectual elites our nations have produced, among other things, the most paramount problem is the question of hunger and/or the inability of our nations to subsist themselves. In most of our nations, for example in Dahomey, poverty has reduced people to "scratching" for the "barest of bare livings". This is an affront to human dignity.

This notwithstanding, rather than seek solution to the hunger problem, most of our "intellectuals" have poignantly chosen that "the only way forward...was to become *scolarisés* - in other words, to convert... into French bourgeois intellectuals."[39]

For this matter, many Dahoméens (and quite frankly many Africans) have fervently pursued the status of being a scolarisé (scholar) just for the sake of it. As I previously mentioned, in my opinion, that is part of the problem rather than part of the solution. Where does it leave the person with the status of *scolarisé* when his nation is languishing in poverty? For one to really earn the status of a *scolarisé* (or a scholarly intellectual) one has to bear in mind that intelligence is a package which comes with the mental and physical aptitude towards problem-solving (be it personally, communally, or nationally).

Jamaica is one of the most educationally-elitist countries in the world in general and Caribbean Island in particular. It is blessed with being one of the world's largest producers of bauxite. Yet, it is languishing in poverty. How much could that nation boast of having more than 95 percent literacy, or "educated elite," or "intellectuals" or "scolarisés", when in fact that nation cannot manage its resources? Congo had been blessed superfluously with copper, cobalt, diamond, uranium, silver, tungsten, columbium, and plutonium. That giant of a nation could not manage its blessings. Then, inconsequential Belgium trampled the giant, and milked what it could.

With all those mineral endowments, Congo never became a developed nation. This is because most of these Third World nations still have metropolitan powers, directly or indirectly, control their resources: Neo-colonialism. If Kuwait and Saudi Arabia could manage their resources, Jamaica could and should. That nation does not have any reason to be poor. The same goes for Nigeria, Ghana, Liberia, Sierra Leone and many other nations abundantly blessed with mineral resources. In view of this, it is my suggestion that a conglomerate of our respective nation's scolarisés (intellectuals), should discuss the issues that threaten the existence of our various nations such as finding ways to pay off the national debts, and ways to avoid the imperialists' snares – IMF and or its other agents. Such intellectuals should also do all they can to effectuate a positive change in our respective nations.

While we may not possibly upgrade our nations to the standard of the developed nations, we could perhaps do something about the hunger ravaging our nations. Mass starvation in a nation is the highest degree of national disgrace, humiliation and shame. It is the last stage of human degradation. Therefore, effective solutions should be sought with immediacy. When this happens, then we can happily wear the cap of a scolarisé without any shadow of a doubt that in deed that's what we are.

Meanwhile, dependency has been the norm in our socio-political life in general and economic life in particular, especially at the national level. In that vein, "flights from traditional staples have led Africa to depend on foreign food growers, and the import bill has contributed to the serious economic crises faced by African countries. whereas 'in 1884 the African lived within an endogenous culture firmly anchored on African soil, African crafts and African cosmographies, the African of 1984 looks to foreign soils, foreign factories, and foreign heavens for bodily and spiritual sustenance."[40]

Based on the above, it could be argued that the contemporary Africans are the ones that tie themselves to the apron-strings of metropolitan nations, thereby making themselves pawns, at will. One of the worst things that could happen to a nation is to propel itself into receiving foreign aids and loans with political and economic strings attached. Such loans and aids are usually wrapped up in ambiguous legal and financial terms that are not easily discernible. We have to avoid such loans. They do more harm than good. If China, which has more than one quarter of the world's population can feed itself, individual African nations also can and should feed their respective populations without making their nations a sacrificial lamb on the altars of neo-imperialism. We have the resources to make it. We only have to tap on those resources.

It is time we turned things around. It is time we controlled our destinies by managing our resources very well. It is time we stopped burying ourselves in debts. It is time we stopped making ourselves pawns at will. It is time we stopped neo-imperialists from neo-colonizing us. It is time we invested in our countries and built our technologies. It is time we paved the way for a better future for our children, and make the path smooth for their posterity. It is time we redeemed our national identity; and put a stop to the negative image we have worn thus far. No continent has been so belittled and so impugned as ours. Make no mistake about it, no person or body of persons (nation or body of nations) can use one (or a nation) as a puppet or a fool, unless one lets them. But one has to first, extricate oneself from any situation that would warrant such a usage. When God created man (us), He gave man charge over his destinies. He said unto man, 'be fruitful and multiply; fill the earth and subdue it. The phrase subdue, here, means develop. Thus, He gave us charge to develop our communities and our nations (the earth); thereby, giving us the wherewithal (natural mineral resources) with which to carry on the assigned task. He did His job making the resources available. Shouldn't we do ours, by putting the resources to the intended effect? Could we not propel our nations to a more sublime economic level? It suffices, here, to say, had the mismanagement etc., happening in our societies today taken place during the Mosaic day, God might not have minded adding the eleventh commandment, forbidding us from defrauding our nations; knowing full well that such exhortation would aid and ensure the continual wealth of our nations which, one way or another, might warranty the eradication of other social vices for which He gave the Ten Commandments.

In conclusion, the awareness of the existence of a problem, is the first step toward finding a solution. First, the nation involved should be able to identify the problem, analyse it, and find an effective solution to it. More pragmatic solutions are usually result-oriented. In other words, the effectiveness of any suggested solutions should be easy to measure, qualitatively or quantitatively. The applicability of the solution, in relation to the problem should also be direct and feasible. Through this process, the African nations could define their problems and whatever else that submerges them, and perpetually deepens them, in Third World economic condition.

Then, they should strive to extricate themselves from such and possibly save themselves from economic squalor and the circle of doom.

Table Box 1: Seventeen Highly Indebted Countries

Country	Debt Outstanding 1987		Debt Service 1987-89 (US$ Billion)		Debt Ratios (%)			Trade Balance (US$ Billion) 1983-87		Average Annual Growth Rates 1980-87 (Percent)			
	Total (US$ Billion)	Private Source (%)	Of which total	Of which interest	DOD/ GNP 1986	Interest/ XGS 1987[c]	Average Value	Annual balance in 82	GDP	Exports	Imports	Investment	Per Capita Consumption
Argentina													
Bolivia[c]													
Brazil													
Chile													
Colombia													
Costa Rica[c]													
Cote d'Ivoire													
Ecuador													
Jamaica													
Mexico													
Morocco													
Nigeria													
Peru													
Philippines													
Uruguay[c]													
Venezuela													
Yugoslavia													
Total													

a. Estimated total external liabilities including use of IMF credit
b. Debt service is based on long-term debt and terms at end 1986. It does not take into account new loans contracted or debt rescheduling signed after that date
c. Based on interest due in 1987 on long-term debt outstanding at the end of 1986, relative to 1966 exports of goods and all services
d. Based on interest due in 1987 on long-term debt outstanding at the end of 1986, relative to 1986 exports of goods and all services
e. Data for 1987 are preliminary estimates. Growth rates (least squares) are computed from time series in constant prices
f. End – 1986 debt
g. Excludes private non-guaranteed debt.

Source: World Debt Tables, External Debt of Developing Countries 1987/88 Edition. Volume 1, Analysis & Summary Tables of the World Bank, Washington DC

CHAPTER FOUR

Remnants of Colonialism

In my opinion, colonialism does not necessarily mean when foreign imperialistic powers maintain a direct or indirect hegemony over a nation and its people. It goes beyond such a narrow scope, and encompasses the indigenous leaders and/or subjects who exploit their nations and hold political, social and economic development in abeyance. Who is doing it does not matter: be it foreign nationals or indigenous ones. So long as exploitation is involved, it is imperialism. So long as it is exploitative, it is imperialism. So long as it is imperialism, it is colonialism -period. On Sunday June 23, 1996, it was captioned on Sixty-Minutes news how Raul Salinas defrauded his nation of $300,000,000.00 two years ago, when his brother, Carlos Salinas was President of Mexico. While his nation is saturated with debt and its citizens are laden with loads of sufferings, he has been busy wiring hundreds of millions of dollars to secrete bank accounts in Switzerland, Britain, Columbia and Citi Bank, New York. Such is what holds most Third World countries at work, encumbering them from development.

Until we exorcise ourselves of the elements of the spirit of exploitation and deride the spirit of fraudulence, until we start investing in our nations and quench the desire to swindle one another, directly or indirectly, we are no better than the imperialists and we are no better than the colonialists for indeed we are imperialists and colonialists. Even worse: for we are re-colonizing ourselves. Until we renascent ourselves and our minds to the benefit of our communities and our nations, remnants of colonialism are still at work in us.

My cousin said,

> That Africans don't have culture!
> That Africans don't have history!
> That Africans don't have religion!
> That Africans don't have language!
> That Africans are not civilized!

My cousin said,

> That it is his duty to extend
> The Arab sphere of influence
> To Africans in Africa...
> And if God helps him to achieve his ambition,
> The whole African continent
> Would become an Arab continent,
> So that Africans would become civilized![41]

> -S. Anai Kelueljang

Even as the Twentieth-century draws to a close, the imperialist adventure which was started by the Arabs since the early 1300s, the Europeans since 1400s, Soviets since 1900s, (all perpetrated on Africa and its peoples) the end of such evil ambition is not yet in sight; nor will it be. Given the hopes and aspirations of such imperialists as the former Prime Minister of Libya, Muammar al-Gaddaffi, the West through debt-trap-peonage via IMF, and self-imposed mishaps via mismanagement, colonialism though perceived dead, is very much alive. And it will stay alive, and will continue to thrive in Africa and other Third World nations wherever it finds a breeding ground, if the people let it.

In spite of the small size of the Great Roman Empire it conquered and ruled the world. As small as Great Britain is, it colonized half the world. But as big as Africa is, it cannot ward-off the imperialist-flies that perched on and tend to suck its phallus dry. As noted by Marcus Garvey, "the greatest weapon used against the Negro is Disorganization." As long as the Africans remain disorganized, the imperialists who are organized will continue to use Africans as pawns. A similar question that was asked in the slave-situation presents itself here: if the Africans should make themselves sacrificial-lamb on the altar of the imperialist, shouldn't their offering be accepted in the hands of the almighty imperialists; shouldn't their meekness be perceived as their weakness?

No continent and its people has suffered the humiliation and degradation Africa has undergone, and still undergoes; and will continue to undergo. If we do not use our brains and our senses, then we would remain stooges to those who do. Little wonder is it, that little Libya, a mere microcosm of the Arab world, would dream of finishing off the imperialist adventure rained on Africa since the Thirteenth-century. The (Nigerian) Guardian, Sunday May 5, 1985, revealed Gaddaffi's inclination (and approach) to convert the entire African nation into an Arab continent. Why shouldn't he dream thus? No one is too small to dream; and no dream is too big for anyone. It is therefore one thing to dream, it is quite another to put it in practice. In Gaddaffi's case, however, he ventured into Chad. Quite a few African nations like Somalia, Egypt, Libya, Morocco, Tunisia, Algeria, etc., have been grabbed by the Arab world. And a few other zombies, may soon follow. Increasing the net grab to over 50 per cent.

The poem above depicted the Africans as people without civilization. Well, the Africans have civilization. They also have brains. They only do not use them. At least, not to their own national advantage. The metropolitan influence has dominated their way of thinking. They do not think about the benefit of their nations. They think about self-gratification at the expense of their nations and in favor of the metropolitan imperialists. The people are civilized. They are also educated. But the people are disorganized, and make their nations easy to be perambulated and exploited through imperialism.

It was also said above that, the Africans have no history. They have one. Five to six hundred years of degradation and deprivation is enough history and enough lessons to learn from. The problem is: the people do not learn a lesson; not from their past. History has revealed that the Negroes (Africans) have had more Moses and many messiahs in the form of Pan-Africanists and Nationalists that have come and gone without success in delivering the Africans from the bondage of imperialism. It is sad to note that if by now the Africans have not learned that they and their continent are endangered species, even if a prophet resurrects from the dead to educate them on their plight, they still may not learn. African people do not learn from their history.

It has often been said, as in the poem above, that Africans have no religion. They do. They just do not value their religion. This topic has been exhausted in chapter two. Because of the imbecilic way they manage their resources; from age to age the Africans have been described as uncivilized. Well, the people are educated and civilized.

They just do not use their education properly. This has been alluded to before, and the topic has been exhausted in chapter three.

We also have seen in chapter three, how some African nations subjected themselves to financial, economic and social obloquy. Should we follow the admonitions of such Pan-Africanists as Marcus Garvey, we should have been able to save ourselves from the evil of imperialism. Here, Marcus Garvey forewarned: The attitude of the white race is to subjugate, to exploit, and if necessary exterminate the weaker peoples with whom they come in contact. They subjugate first, if the weaker-peoples will stand for it; then exploit, and if they will not stand for subjugation, the other recourse is extermination.[42]

What the Arab imperialists, the European colonialists, and the American neo-colonialists have, heretofore, visited upon Africa confirms Garvey's theory. He went on to advise those of us who suffer from a spirit of subservience to the interests of whites: to always remember "that the Jew in his political and economic urge is always first a Jew; the white man is first a white man under all circumstances, and you can do no less than being first and always a Negro, and all else will take care of itself. Let no one inoculate you with evil doctrines to suit their own conveniences. There is no humanity before that which starts with yourself, 'Charity begins at home.'[43]

And to those of us who lack self-confidence he exhorted: "Negroes the world over must practice one faith, that of Confidence in themselves, with One God: One Aim: One Destiny: Let no religious scruples, no political machination divide us, but let us hold together under all climes and in every country."[44] Had we learned that exultation only comes from self-confidence, the IMF blunder (as mentioned in chapter three) could have been avoided.

Marcus Garvey further said: As far as Negroes are concerned, in America we have the problem of lynching, peonage and disfranchisement. In the West Indies, South and Central America we have the problem of peonage, serfdom, industrial and political and governmental inequality. In Africa we have not only peonage and serfdom, but outright slavery, racial exploitation and alien political monopoly. We cannot allow a continuation of these against our race.[45] These things should not continue to happen to the African race, unless that race allows such to continue happening.

Similarly, W, E. B. Du Bois lamented: "I am frightened by the so-called friends who are flocking to Africa. Negro Americans trying to make money from your toil, white Americans who seek by investment and high interest to bind you in serfdom to business as the Near East is bound and as South America is struggling with. For this, America is tempting your leaders, bribing your scholars, and arming your soldiers,"[46]

It is quite a puzzle as to why other races walk all over the African, Does the African let this happen or he doesn't know it is happening? Until the African refutes the appellation of imbecility, other parts of the world would continue to deride, and take advantage of the African. Until the Africans show their docility and, thereby, prove they have learned their lessons and march onward to societal economic self-actualization, the African is still colonized. It is about time the edentulous giant awakened from its dormancy and/or slumber.

In the politico-economic spectrum, African nations are still in an era of suspended animation. At the rate things are going till the next half a century, or more, that continent may never achieve a techno-industrial height nor a politico-economic manhood. Its backwardness, knowingly or unknowingly, accounts for why Africa, a giant of a continent, was, and still is, used as a footstool by "little Belgium, inconsequential Portugal, fourth-rate Spain, resurgent Italy and so on down the line."[47]

Is Africa a giant for nothing? No. A thousand times no. Does it exist for naught? No. A thousand times no. When then will the Africans stop the Arabs; stop the Europeans; stop Americans from walking all over the African? This can only be done when the African stops defrauding his own nation; rebuilds his own nation; and develops his own nation.

Is the African incapable of self-rule? No. A thousand times no. Is the African lacking in political capacity? No. "It cannot be. If the Negro race produced a State which has existed from eons past, it cannot be logical to conclude that that race lacks political capacity.

"Is it because they are lacking in political acumen? Probably so. Most of those who are the self-professed leaders of the various sections of ... Africa are, in reality, and at all due deference to them, worthy of one piece of job, that is, to commit felo-de-se.

In all sincerity, probity and candor, "the main reason why the shibboleth of the inferiority of the African for social and political capacity lingers, is due to the imbecility of most of African leaders or rulers. The word is not so musical to the ear, but it is the truth. After struggling to accumulate wealth, those who succeed, instead of using the same for the benefit of reconstructing their shattered national heritage, use the same" for their personal advantage."[48]

The African asks for leaders, not selfish prating cliques, The African asks for leaders, not mediocre personalities. The African asks for leaders. Yes. Leaders who would be an emblem of statehood. Leaders who would be an emblem of nationalism.

Leaders who would be an emblem of altruism. Leaders who would solve the African problems and deliver the African dreams. Yes. The African is asking for leaders (not rulers). Yes. The African is asking for selfless leaders, not selfish rulers.

But, what does he get? He gets so-called rulers who "perch on altars defiled with the stench of corruption, chicanery, egocentrism, tribal prejudice, cowardice, get-rich-quick philosophy, alphabetimania, and the relics of Uncle Tomism.

"The youth of Africa believe that the time is at hand when they should make a re-evaluation of their raison d'être on this continent. Are Africans created to serve as slaves forever or are they destined to impress their civilization on the world as they had done in the past?"[49] Until Africans in general and their leaders in particular take up the adore of their nations, until they understand that: East, West, North, and South-Home is the best, until they become God-fearing and selfless, and until they relentlessly rebuild their nations, the remnants of colonialism is still in our milieu. Now, the African leaders are the ones colonizing the Africans.

CHAPTER FIVE

The Need to Decolonize the People

Although Africa has been politically decolonized, Africans have yet to' decolonize their minds; and exorcise themselves of the spirit of inferiority. Until we begin to have confidence in ourselves: and begin to realize that: black man is equally talented as whites, that: all things made by whites are no better than those made by blacks; until we exorcise ourselves of that spirit of psychological bondage, mental servitude and socioeconomic thraldom, we are still colonized. Until we emancipate ourselves from such self-enslavement, we remain, an amorphous mass.

The political Decolonization of Africa arose from the realization of African nationalists of what the colonialists were doing to the colonies by way of exploitation, both direct and indirect. The nationalists were, perhaps, also concerned about the influence of colonialism on the African culture and way of life. Under colonialism, all aspects of the peoples' life were openly and directly influenced. Thus, African lifestyle has now, more or less, anchored on European lifestyle. For the most part, social life has rapidly transformed from endogenous to exogenous, making it possible for the metropolitan powers to still maintain imperialist hegemony on Africa and its people till this day. Although it had happened continually for five centuries, the enormity with which African treasure (and resources) were being siphoned to the colonialists' countries of Europe (England, France, Belgium, Portugal, Spain, Italy, Denmark, Holland, Sweden, Brandenburg, etc.) was quite alarming and had beckoned the attention of the nationalists. Something had to be done to stop it. The situation had called for greater promptitude in its stoppage, than for more rhetoric.

No doubt, the Africans were in deadly-slumber for five centuries during which their resources were exhumed. As though awakened by divine-call (like Samuel), nationalist leaders sprang up almost simultaneously from the nooks and crannies of the African continent, with a unanimity of purpose: A struggle for national freedom. This struggle was necessary because: factors of imperialism have continually stultified the normal growth of Africans in the community of nations. The nationalists had deemed it necessary to struggle, to redeem Africa and the black race from the chasms of colonial depredation. They had deemed it necessary to struggle, to redeem the African from political servitude for they had realized that the African race has continually presented a sorry spectacle of degraded humanity. They had to struggle to purge the opprobrious stigma attached to the African race.

These men of honour had deemed it necessary to struggle for our political freedom. They had realized that politically the African had been dominated by alien races and had continually been denied the basic human rights.

Most of these nationalists had been to the white man's countries and had witnessed that socially, the black race within and without Africa has been subjected to inexplicable discrimination of various types both in Africa and abroad. They had to put up a struggle, to eradicate such injustice, to the best of their abilities.

In the economic spectrum, the nationalists saw it wise to struggle and rescue the African who has been subjected to exploitation of a most heinous type, whilst he vegetates below the minimum subsistence level of existence.

The struggle was necessary. It was inevitable. It was a sine qua non. The nationalists were further motivated in the struggle for self-determination when they realized that Britain and the United States had engaged Africans in World War II, in an effort to garner freedom for the white man. After the war, the struggle for self-determination intensified. The drive was: if the African had just fought a war of freedom for the white man, how justifiable would it be for the same white man not to give the African his political freedom? With such drive and determination, the nationalists surged ahead to redeem their nations from political bondage, and provide a place in the sun for the people.

The above summed the guiding spirit under which fathers of African independence such as Nnamdi Azikiwe, Obafemi Awolowo, Abubakar Tafawa Balewa of Nigeria, Kwame Nkrumah of Ghana, Julius Nyerere of Tanzania, Kenneth Kaunda of Zambia, Jomo Kenyatta of Kenya, etc., most of whom were alumni of metropolitan universities in the United States and Europe, stirred the continent into a political ebullition as they struggled to put an end to the imperialists' excavating and expatriating of Africa's wealth.

Having smelled and tasted racism in the metropolitan west during their student years, they returned to their respective nations and eventually, much like Moses, led their people out of the bondage of colonialism, at least, politically speaking.

Nevertheless, one may argue that by the middle of the nineteenth century Britain had already "wished to abandon British colonies (including the Gold Coast) on the grounds that they were not worth holding."[50] This line of reasoning, however, is as misleading as it is rippled with prevarication. A more succinct argument will be interposed: if Britain had tended to abandon the colonies because "they were not worth holding," why did they (the colonialists) maintain their hold for centuries? On the other hand, if they really had the proclivity to do so, then, it must have been because by the middle of the nineteenth century, five centuries of continuous exploitation, excavation and expatriation of African wealth had left little or nothing "worth holding" on to.

Besides, even when Britain had begun to relinquish some of its colonies, France was still intent at expanding its.

Whatever the case may be, the efforts of the nationalists paid off in the late 1950s and early 1960s when self-rule started to displace colonial-rule. Ghana, for instance, won her political independence on March 6, 1957, under the premiership of Kwame Nkrumah, who subsequently became the countries first president when it became a Republic on July 1, 1960. Ghana, therefore, became the first African nation, within the British Commonwealth, to attain self-governance. This was largely because Ghana had an early formation of political parties; thanks to the ex-servicemen from World War II who played an enormous role in such a formation. The first political organization was formed, and led, by Joseph Danquah whose political party was the United Party. Nkrumah used to belong to this party, but later broke away, and formed his own party, Convention People's Party (CPP). The CPP soon came out as the best organized of the country's political movements. Thus, in the referendum that followed, Nkrumah's CPP emerged victorious capturing 1,016,076 votes whilst his opponent, Joseph B. Danquah, leader of Opposition Unity Party (UP), gathered only 124,623 votes, on a 54 percent poll.

Unfortunately, soon after Nkrumah's assumption of office, negative events started happening that subsequently brought about his demise. Soon after the attainment of independence, there developed a conflict between the Government and the regional chiefs, who, by tradition, were the religious, political and military leaders of their peoples. Also, there grew suspicion among Nkrumah's opponents, that his administration was tending "towards dictatorship." Chief among the reasons for such a suspicion were:

a) Nkrumah's provision in the Constitution (published May 6, 1960) for the eventual surrender of Ghana's sovereignty, in whole or in part, to a Union of African States (as evidenced in his memoir - Africa Must Unite).

b) The Constitution had also made a provision for an extensive amount of powers given to the President. The functions of Head of State and Head of Government were combined. The president was given the power to veto legislation, to dissolve the National Assembly, and to appoint the Judiciary. As though these were not enough,

c) On August 23, 1960, the Criminal Code Bill was enacted, giving the President powers to impose press censorship, and to restrict the importation of publications deemed "contrary to public interest". Then, on May 1, 1961, President, Dr. Nkrumah, stating that the country was entering a "new political revolution regarding the struggle for the total liberation of the African continent, and that his actions were necessary in order to lead Ghana into "a new phase of the industrial and technical revolution,"

d) Assumed the posts of General Secretary of the party and that of Chairman of the central committee. Furthermore,

e) On June 4, 1961, he took over the direct responsibility for Ghana's main development program. Also,

f) On July 22, the country's broadcasting system came under his direct supervision.

g) On September 22, he became the Supreme Commander of the Armed forces, and replaced British Army Officers in the Ghanaian forces with Ghanaians. And the Armed forces came to his direct command, effective August 31, 1965.

h) On November 4, 1963, he passed a Bill (Preventive Detention Act) with the proclivity to silence his opponents even more. This Act, specifically, targeted many leaders and supporters of the Opposition Party.

i) He made it illegal to oppose the government; and on November 3, 1961, a Bill was passed, extending the Jurisdiction of Ghanaian courts to offenses committed even outside the country. Finally,

j) On February 22, 1964, a Bill was passed, giving Nkrumah the power to remove any Judge of the Supreme Court or, of the High Court any time he felt he had "sufficient reasons" to do so.

k) Following a unanimous vote of 96.5 per cent poll in favor of the proposal, Ghana became a one-party State on February 21, 1964. Thus, CPP became the only legitimate political party.

Of course, Nkrumah could not do this for so long without having people raise their eyebrows. The power to tamper with the Judiciary which he conferred upon himself, provoked sentiments in certain opponents such as Joseph Danquah who, on December 11, 1960, pronounced that President Nkrumah had dealt the last fatal blow at Ghana's first experiment with parliamentary democracy. Upon hearing such a pronouncement, instead of making amends, Nkrumah tightened screws on his opponents. For instance, members of the former Opposition Party were, thenceforth, prohibited from occupying the front benches on Nkrumah's left.

Things deteriorated further. Following the discovery of an alleged plot to assassinate Dr. Kwame Nkrumah on October 3, 1961, some important members of the Opposition group, including Dr. Joseph Danquah, Mr. Joe Appiah (deputy leader of the Opposition group), were arrested. They became the first to experience a baptism of fire under the Preventive Detention Act. During this period, strikes had broken out in such places as Takoradi, Sekondi, Accra and Kumasi in protest against rises in the cost of living which was caused by the introduction of austerity measures in the budget on July 4 and 7, 1961.

On June 20, 1962, Dr. Joseph Danquah was released, and got re-arrested on January 8, 1964 following another allegation that there was a new attempt on the life of the President, which was alleged to have occurred on January 2, 1964. On February 4, 1965, Dr. J. B. Danquah died in prison. The official claim was that he died of "heart failure." However, Dr. Kofi A. Busia, another government Opposition, and former leader of the United Party, had alleged that Dr. Danquah had died out of ill-treatment and torture dealt to political prisoners.

On February 21, 1964, Ghana became a one-party State, following a unanimous vote of 96.5 per cent poll in favor of the proposal; thereby, making CPP the only lawful party. Nonetheless, there was no way Nkrumah's proposal could have had such a high rate of approval, in spite of all the Oppositions he had had. The only logical probability could have arisen iron his having suppressed his opponents. For example, there shouldn't be any wonder that when nominations were had on July 1, 1965, not only were CPP candidates the only ones nominated, but they returned unopposed. Consequently, on June 10, 1965, Nkrumah was unanimously elected President for the second five-year term, by the new Parliament.

When most or all of the functions of the government are consolidated in a person, or body of persons, it paves the way for tyranny. Kwame Nkrumah's regime was nothing short of this allusion. Power corrupts. And absolute power corrupts, absolutely. With Nkrumah garnering all the powers he could muster, his administration was rapidly tending towards despotism. On September 28, 1961, he expelled six members of his Government including two Cabinet ministers in the persons of Mr. Kojo Botsio and K. A. Gbedemah. In the same vein, he had forced six other members of his Government to surrender parts of their personal assets to the Government. Soon after, these political victims were stripped of their rights and privileges as party members.

Following this same line of odious treatment, on August 29, 1962, the executive Secretary, Mr H. H. Cofie-Crabbe, the Information Minister, Mr. Tawiah Adamafio, and the Foreign Minister, Mr. Ako Adjei, were all detained, under the Preventive Detention Act. The reason given for such execrable act was that it was done "in the interests of the security of the State;" then, they were charged with treason in connection with alleged assassination attempt on Nkrumah.

However, the Court presided over by Sir Arku Korsah, acquitted all three men on December 9. Nkrumah, of course, did not like this; therefore, he discharged Sir Korsah as being the Chief Justice of Ghana, effective, immediately. No reason was given for such a dismissal. Then, on December 23, Nkrumah passed a Bill giving the President (i.e., himself) power to annul decisions of the Court. And declared the acquittals of those men, null and void.

At the same time, Ghana was having political problems with Great Britain, the United States, Germany, and even its neighbouring country, Togo. All these countries were alleged to have had activities with subversive intentions against Ghana. However, his glory as the President of Ghana waned and Nkrumahism collapsed when he was deposed (through a military coup led by Major General Joseph

A. Ankrah) on February 24, 1966, while he was on a visit to the Communist China in quest of seeking peace for Vietnam.

Pursuers of political independence, should after realizing it, either sink or swim with it. Whatever they opt to do with it, one thing is clear: "Human beings resist force anywhere and will not imbibe for so long anything done out of coercion."[51] This is as true in Ghana as it is anywhere else. Idi Amin's Uganda crystallizes this precept. Or, was it that of his predecessor, Apollo Milton Obete? Dr. Obete's regime, though much better than that of Idi Amin, still left Ugandans wondering what else is in the game of politics but despotism.

Obete, having led his party, the Uganda People's Congress (UPC) to victory in the national referendum on April 25,1962, formed his Government; which, much like Nkrumah's Ghana, tended to proscribe the growth of other political parties, and form a one-party socialist State.

Yet, much like Nkrumah, Obete assumed full powers of the government and embarked on arbitrary imprisonment of even members of his Government, For example, on February 22, 1966, right after assuming the powers of the government, he imprisoned five Cabinet Ministers for no justifiable reason, pending official "investigation" into their activities.

Getting more and more drunk with power, on March 2, 1966, Obete usurped both the powers of the President and Prime Minister. Whoever has seen a monolithic parliamentary system of government, where the functions of the President and that of the Prime Minister are combined in a person, has seen a peremptorily devious government, A semblance of sinisterly occurrences comparable to that of Nkrumah's Ghana took place in Obete's Uganda. Obete, much like Nkrumah, repressed all opposition by force, compelling the former opposition leader, Kabaka of Bugandi, to flee the country.

He lived in exile, in London, till he died on November 21, 1969. Kabaka and the other fellows mentioned afore were not the only ones to taste a baptism of fire in Obete's regime. In 1967, 22 persons (which included one woman) were detained based on an allegation that they plotted to assassinate President Apollo Obete and his Ministers.

Whether the allegation was true or false, there seemed to be insufficient evidence to buttress it. Thus, the accused were discharged. Nevertheless, a real attempt was made on Obete's life on December 19 of 1969.

Following this, the existence of all parties, except Uganda People's Congress (the ruling party of Obete) became banned; and on May 6, 1970, six of the culprits were sentenced to life imprisonment for the role they played in the assassination attempt.

Also, much like Nkrumah confiscated personal assets, Obete though on a wider spectrum, under his "Common Man's Charter," nationalized privately owned undertakings. Under the same Charter, he nationalized all import and export trades, with the exception of oil and/or petroleum products. In the same vein, he promulgated the acquisition of 60 per cent share holdership in public transport companies, plantation industries, oil companies, banks, copper mining and manufacturing industries. As his governance tended more and more toward dictatorship, it lost its popularity. On January 25, 1971, he was ousted by military coup, led by Major General Idi Amin.

A closer observation of the ascension to, and declination from, the political independence of another country such as Guinea, under Sekou Touré, will reveal similar symptoms of tyranny which, believe it or not, was to blame for the stultification of the true meaning of the phrase: political independence.

Sekou Touré was no less despotic than his Ghanaian, or Ugandan, counterparts. Nor were the sufferings he bequeathed to his subjects less comparable to those visited upon the Biblical Job. Although there should not be a platform, nor a yard-steak, with which to measure and/ or compare sufferings, whether it was entered into by Job, or by any other human element, the Guinean experience under Sekou Touré was nothing short of a baptism of fire. While Touré theorized that human element could achieve "success" through suffering, conventional wisdom presupposes that human beings achieve far less than their marginal potential, when in suffering state. Besides, what has sufferings got to do with political and economic development? I have searched for answers pertaining to this, and found none that makes more sense than Chinweizu's. In his opinion, "the notion of development through suffering is intellectually silly, and in the unfortunate event of its being put into practice, it inevitably reveals its bankruptcy by producing even more suffering."[52] Such a bankruptcy was evident in the results which manifested in Sekou Touré's program. The sufferings, which were entered upon them, encumbered them from any iota of progress. Did not Sekou Touré know that his theory was anything but astute? Did he not know that his subjects were scorching and toiling under a program which was nothing but a lampoon? Did he not capriciously imbibe his subjects in destitution because it gratified his mind to see them wallowing and clamoring in such a squalor? What more could spell tyranny, if Guineans1 plights didn't? How much more tyrannical could one be, when, as a father-figure, one hands stones to those who cry for bread, and scorpions to those asking for meat? In essence, that is precisely what is happening in our society where and when people sought deliverance from political bondage, only to have those who promised them such deliverance extinguish the lights in the middle of nowhere, and subject them to unfathomable rancor. In the Guinean situation, "Despite a fine beginning, despite an enormous mobilization of popular will and enthusiasm for a brave adventure to independence and prosperity, Guinea got nowhere. In 26 years of suffering, success never bothered to come their way."[53] When they opted for independence, which they received on October 2, 1958, following their rejection of the new Constitution of the Fifth Republic of France which was handed down to them on September 28, they had hoped for a messiah who would deliver them from imperial political demagoguery. Their rejection of the French-made Constitution buttressed their inclination. When Touré, who had till that moment been Prime Minister, assumed office as Head of the first Government de la République, the people were not only enthusiastic but gave him their maximum support.

Much like his counterparts in Uganda and Ghana, Touré piloted the nation to a socialist, one-party State, wherein, the existence of all other parties were banned, except the ruling Parti Démocratique de Guinée (PDG), which was Guinea's part of the Rassemblement Démocratique Africain (RDA). In February of 1968, Touré announced that his "Maxist" government would get more strict in attacking the vestiges of imperialism, capitalism, tribalism, and religion. Thenceforth, torture, imprisonment and execution, became part of his credo. On January 24, 1971, a Supreme Revolutionary Tribunal set up by the Guinean National Assembly sentenced 92 Africans to death; and 72 others were sentenced to life imprisonment with hard labour; a Roman Catholic Archbishop, Mgr. Raymond-Marie Tchidimbo and two German ex-officio were included in this group.

Also, following a subversive attempt to overthrow his regime, which was allegedly plotted by Portugal and other unnamed foreign powers, forty persons were convicted, thirteen of which were sentenced to death, while twenty-seven others were sentenced to life imprisonment with hard labor. On March 31, 1967, he expelled all European missionaries implementing what he called "Cultural Revolution". Included in his list of discipline was a Roman Catholic Archbishop, whom he expelled for opposing his idea of nationalizing all Churches in Guinea.

What nationalization of Churches had to do with revamping the colonial-battered economy beats my imagination. Instead of focusing on what to do to restructure the economic base of the nation, Sekou Touré put all his effort in attempting to stamp out crime, bribery, corruption, prostitution, street begging, depredation and other social vices. Much like many other African leaders, "he believed development could be better tackled later on....Such mundane things as roads, farms, markets, well-stocked shops – all had to wait till virtue had been stamped into the Guinean populace."[54] The irony is that leaders with that kind of assumption loud to forget that they had it in a reversed form.

Lots of social vices are naturally petered out with a buoyant economy. However, Touré believed his country should first go through the furnace of fire, and pass through the eye of the needle before pursuing economic threshold.

After thwarting the coup attempt, Sekou Touré tightened the screws and sealed the country's borders to prevent citizens from escaping. Then he continually hammered and preached his gospel of moral virtues. "He confiscated their money... he created an efficient spy network for detecting deviations and dissent from that program of rigorous righteousness which, he seemed to believe, the mysterious dialectic of the universe would reward with development."[55]

Touré was in power for twenty-six years, and, much like most African rulers (or leaders), did practically nothing for economic improvement. Roads were unpaved and full of pot-holes; per capita income plummeted. All he did was mere rhetoric; preaching, preaching, and some more preaching regarding moral virtue. Sekou Touré, the apostle of moral virtue, was not even walking his talk and practicing his preaching. While he burdened Guineans with mountains of sufferings, he was all those years enjoying himself. That physician should have first healed himself of his own moral maladies, before preaching about moral virtues to the public. By the same token, Robert Gabriel Mugabe was a Zimbabwean revolutionary politician. He served Zimbabwe as a Prime Minister from 1980 to 1987 (a period of 7 years), and then as a President from 1987 to 2017 (a period of 30 years). He was ousted and died on September 6, 2019 in Gleneagles Hospital, Singapore at the age of 95 years. That Mugabe died in a foreign hospital signified that for 37 years during which he was a political leader of Zimbabwe, he never built a single hospital where he could receive medical treatment. Similar thing is currently happening in Nigeria, where President Muhammadu Buhari frequents hospitals in London, England, for medical reasons. This indicates that hospitals in Nigeria lack basic amenities, equipment, and infrastructure.

In the Third World countries in general and Africa in particular, there are many "leaders (actually rulers) like Sekou Touré, who approach development as if it was a redemptive passage from purgatory. Such leaders are operating from a feudal, theological, paternalistic and magical world outlook; whatever their delusions, they are not addressing their people's economic problems, but rather some problems, probably psychological, of their own. As we all know, priests who recommend sacrifice usually do not include themselves among what should be sacrificed; for they usually have their eyes on the carcasses left on the altar. As for the sheep that are to be sacrificed, they usually do not have a say in selecting the rites."[56]

Ghana got its independence in 1957. Guinea got its independence in 1958, and Nigeria got its independence in 1960. It is now about sixty years since most African countries got their independence. Had African leaders or rulers concentrated on economic development since all these years, Africa would not be as economically decrepit as it is today. The sacrificial lambs are the ones suffering, not the offerers. If the leaders are bearing the brunt of the sufferings as borne by the subjects, they would have understood and may have done something to change the economic situations.

When one compares colonial administration with indigenous administration, one wonders which is better. No doubt, no one would choose bondage to freedom. However, considering that colonialist administration was tottered and thrown out because of exploitation, only to be replaced with indigenous despots and exploiters, one wonders which way to go. "Were the Guinean population given a say in their development strategy," of course, they would not choose the route of "endless sacrifices and suffering."[57]

Suffering, in whatever degree (be it big or small), is never an option chosen by the citizens of any nation. However, it is deliberately handed down to them, whether they like it or not.

When Africans opted for political freedom, they hoped to get with it, other social amenities and economic niceties that would help accord them individual happiness, stop exploitation, and give their nations bountiful wealth. When these dreams are far-fetched, even in the midst of plenty, one wonders which way to go. With the forgoing in mind, one could say that Africa is still colonized in a dichotomous fashion. First; (directly) by those indigenous African leaders who hold the nations back from economic development. And second: (indirectly) by metropolitan imperialists – through peonage. It behoves me to ask: when will the salvation come? Shall our nations stay in bondage till the end of time? Shall our nations stay undeveloped for how many more centuries?

When will our roads be paved? When will our shelves be stocked with cornucopia of foods? When shall we have a concourse of infrastructure at our disposal? When shall we have pipe-borne water in every household? When shall we have steady electricity; and clean sanitary environment? May African leaders try to put the natural resources to work. May they help their respective countries achieve the maximum economic potential. May they pursue the altruistic goals and objectives of their respective nations, thereby instilling hopes, aspirations and dignity in Africans rather than pursuing selfish, individualistic goals. May the leaders be selfless, and help Africans in actualizing the African Dream. In this I pray. Selah.

CHAPTER SIX

Military Politics
(A Myth or A Reality?)

A modern State is not built for the pleasure of building it.
It is not an end in itself.
We must keep ourselves from the love of power,
which makes a god of the State, crushing man under it.

Leopold Sedar Senghor

Military intervention in civil politics is a cankerworm that has eaten so deep into the fabric of African polity. Here, "the monopoly of the legitimate use of physical force is part of the very definition of the modern state."[58]

It was a learned behavior from the remnants of the colonial legacy - ruling by force. The only difference here is, this time it is the military, the African military, usurping power by means of coups and - ruling by force. The first time the military got into the arena of African politics was in 1960 with "the mutiny of the Force publique in the Congo...and in December 1960 the Imperial Guard in Ethiopia made an attempt to overthrow the Emperor."[59] Subsequent ones took place in Dahomey and Togo in 1963.

In fact, "between January 1963 and the end of February 1966 there were fourteen significant cases of political intervention by the military. By early 1968 there had been nineteen successful military coups and by the end of 1970 the total number of relevant major incidents...was near to thirty."[60]

The military intervenes in civil polity for a number of reasons. It could be in an attempt "to gain acceptance as potentially legitimate national leaders."[61] In pre-independence Africa and shortly afterwards, the military was looked down upon - with disgust - and mercilessly without regard. This was so because in those days as conventional education was a novelty, there was shortage of well-educated recruits. People had regarded soldiers as illiterates and nothing but an amorphous mass. Some of these soldiers had been in foreign services during the two world wars. At home, they had been treated with disregard as issues facing veterans were rarely, if ever, discussed excepting in 1948, when Commandant Henri Ligier attempted to set up a commission to inquire into and take care of veterans' affairs in French West Africa. Thus, the search for identity and the desire to command respect could have prompted the African soldier to teach the civilian to bow before the man behind the barrel of the gun. In contemporary Africa, however, the officers are now well-trained and educated. Sometimes most of them even have up to college or university education, as was the case of Colonel Ojukwu, in Nigeria, who switched from civil service to the military in 1957 despite his university education.

The ethos of military in politics has been guarded with one reason after another. It should be mentioned perhaps in parenthesis that a chunk of African soldiers received quite a substantial amount of University education ranging from the then Imperial College to the London School of Economics to the Royal Military Academy. The last of these three is known to have produced more heads of state in Africa and India as almost has been the case with the second. For example, General Aguiyi-Ironsi, Hassan Kastina, David Ejoor, Major Chukwuma Nzeogwu, General A.. A.. Afrifa, and Major–General A. K. Acran, were all alumni of the Royal Military Academy. Also trained in Britain were Lt. Colonel Yakubu Gowon, Colonel Juxon-Smith of Sierra Leone; and Lt. Colonel Ckwuemeka Odumegwu Ojukwu, who graduated from Oxford University. The respect-issue should therefore not be accepted as a good reason for the coups and military presence in politics. This raises the curious mind of a close observer as to what really is the raison d'être of a nation's army. If it's duty is to defend the statehood of its country against external and internal chaos, should it suffice to use the later as a legitimate reason to be in power, as was the case in Ghana wherein Major-General A. K. Acran cited defense against internal problems as the reason for Nkrumah's oust. According to him, such was necessary "if Ghana was to regain her lost prestige; if she was to return to sanity; if she was not to become a base for communists; if Ghanaians were not to go hungry; if the country was not to collapse morally and financially; in sum, if the country was not to commit national suicide."[62] In the preface of his book "A Myth is Broken", he says:

> Amongst the armies of British Commonwealth countries, with the exception of a few, the idea of a coup d'état is taboo and I believe that, if following Ghana's independence up to the early 1960s, anyone had told me that West African Commonwealth countries would be among the exceptions, I would have doubted not only his political wisdom but also his familiarity with the traditions of armies of these countries.

The above citation is an obvious indication that the military knows full well that its presence in national politics is not only an aberration but a taboo. Should the military be overwhelmed with the desire to do so, they should subject themselves to national referendum or election, and let the people decide.

Some other trivial reasons such as envy and the desire to rule could also be cited as motivating factors for military intervention. Envy was the case in Ivory Coast wherein in 1973 during the presidency of Houphouet-Boigny, despite the existence of relative degree of peace and stability a coup plot was carried out by the soldiers who "looked with envy at the performance of their contemporaries in neighbouring

Upper Volta, Mali, Togo and Dahomey.[63] Sometimes there are not solid reasons for military takeover. A simple misunderstanding following an election is enough reason for the military to usurp power. This happened in 1967 in Sierra Leone after the general election. The final results of that election "were never officially announced. Immediately after the swearing-in of Mr. Stevens as Prime Minister on March 21, he and the Governor-General, Sir Henry J. Lightfoot-Boston, were detained on the orders of the Army Chief, Brigadier David Lansana, who declared martial law."[64] Two days later, the military took over the government, and arrested all the politicians.

Or, it could be an overzealous military, interested in weeding out a civil but autocratic rule, as happened in Uganda, when on January 25, 1971, Dr. Apollo Milton Obete's one-party government was overthrown and replaced by a more vicious and barbarous military regime of Major-General Idi Amin. Yet, in some other instance it could be a vigilante army officer who is eager to protect his national interests from Western influence as could be argued in the case of Colonel Gaddafi of Libya who assumed office on July 21, 1970 and soon after confiscated all Italian assets as an attack on Italian colonialism. In his own words he had written:

"Our souls were in revolt against the backwardness enveloping our country and its land, whose best gifts and riches were being lost through blunder...."[65]

Besides the above reasons, the military may get into the polity in an attempt to quell regional political rivalries as was the case in Nigeria, which prompted the coups of 1966, paving the way for military leadership. This will be discoursed shortly. Whatever the reasons for the intervention, military rule in Africa is now, more or less, the norm rather than an aberration. Not that the people like it. However, it is now the only known administrative establishment in Nigeria. Since after its attainment of independence in 1960, there have been only two serious attempts at civil democratic rule which both ended in coups and counter coups.

The first emergence of the military in the political arena was on January 15, 1966 when young southern military officers such as Major

Adewale-Ademoyega, Major Emmanuel Ifeajuna, Captain Nwobosi, Lt.-Colonel Ojukwu, Major Chukwuma Nzeogwu, etc., carried out a coup d'etat in an effort to extirpate what they saw as corrupt politicians. In Nzeogwu's own words when he went on Radio Kaduna on the afternoon of January 15, 1966 he declared: "The aim of the Revolutionary Council is to establish a strong, united and prosperous nation free from corruption and internal strife.

Our enemies are the political profiteers, the swindlers, the men in the high and low places that seek bribes"⁶⁶ A quick glance at the coup seems it was an Ibo affair as majority of the coup-plotters were Igbos and the politicians killed were mainly non-Ibos.

However, when examined more critically, one could succinctly argue that it was not an Ibo affair. In fact "the plotters had originally planned to kill all regional premiers, including the Igbos: Okpara in the East and Osadebay in the Mid-West."⁶⁷ Perhaps by accident or mere stroke of luck, when his counterparts Tafawa Balewa, Ahmadu Bello, Saduana of Sokoto, Okotie-Eboh, Akintola, etc., were killed, the President, Nnamdi Azikiwe was on convalescence in Britain. Okpara was not killed because of the confusion in Enugu, where he was the premier. But Lt.-Colonel Unegbu, an Igbo, who was the Quartermaster-General at army headquarters was killed by Major Ifeajuna (another Ibo) who was later killed by the Biafrans who believed that he was sabotaging Ojukwu in the secession process. Besides, Nzeogwu was not an Igbo in principle. He was born in the Mid-West, and took the North as his home. He was fluent in Hausa, and his closest friends were from among the northerners. At his death, the Federal troops made sure they recovered his corpse and buried him in Kaduna, with full military honors for he was seen as a true Nigerian patriot. Also, Major Ademoyega was not an Igbo. He was a Yoruba officer. Equally, Lt Colonel Victor Adebukunola Banjo was a Yoruba officer.

They were actively involved in the coup as were the Igbo officers. Nevertheless, Major–General J. T. Umunnakwe Aguiyi-Ironsi who led the counter coup was an Igbo. That notwithstanding, it would be an assumption undulated with fallacy to call the coup an Igbo one.

Before the first coup, there really was a great deal of strife, violence and civil unrest which ensued in Western Nigeria as a result of the elections held on October 11, 1965 in which the electoral officers were accused of irregular conduct; "new impetus was given to the riots and demonstrations directed against the Regional Government when the Chairman of the Federal Electoral Commission announced in November that grave irregularities had occurred during the elections."[68] The UPGA, Chief Akintola's party was accused by the Opposition Action Group (Chief Awolowo's party), of rigging the election thereby making it possible for Akintola to be re-elected. The riots therefore were a major contributor to the first coup mentioned above. After the coup, the politicians handed the country's administration over to the Army and the police under the control of General Aguiyi-Ironsi, the then Supreme Commander of the Armed forces.

General Ironsi was killed on July 29, 1966, at Ibadan during the second military coup carried out by the northern military dissidents who were not satisfied with the outcome of the first coup wherein they believed only the northerners were killed. On August 1, Lt.-Colonel Yakubu Gowon, the Army chief of Staff, announced that he had taken over control of Nigeria. This was the beginning of a bigger problem. Within about a year, relations between the Federal Government and the Eastern Region began to deteriorate. As things began to grow worse between the Federal Government and the Eastern Region, a great number of the Igbos in various parts of the country, especially in the North and West, were being massacred. Following the obfuscation in relations between the Federal Government and the Eastern Region, Lt.-Colonel Odumegwu Ojukwu, the Governor of Eastern Region threatened to secede. On May 30, 1967, he declared the Republic of Biafra.

To crush the secession of Biafra, the Federal Government under the leadership of Yakubu Gowon, received massive military aid from Britain and Communist countries with which he built "military superiority"[69] and waged a-three-year war with Odumegwu Ojukwu. During the war, millions of Ibos died; many as a result of kwashiorkor – which resulted from lack of food and the essential nutrients as the Biafrans were cut off from food supply amidst fighting a three year war with little or no arms. Needless to say, the world watched while the genocide took place much in the same way as it did watch and look-on in 1994 while a similar genocide replicated itself in Rwanda. Without doubt, "if such a tragedy were taking place in the middle of Europe rather than among black Africans, Anglo-American society would be convulsed with demands for action."[70]

Whatever the case may be, credit must be given to the International Red Cross organization for their effort in trying to fly in relief through Fernando Po albeit the fact that their effort was frustrated by the failure of the two warring factions on reaching a consensus on the methods of transportation and distribution of the relief in question.

While the Federal Government insisted on having the relief go through its territory to Biafra, the Biafran leaders were understandably suspicious that the relief might be poisoned en-route and therefore insisted on an alternate avenue. The humanitarian effort of the International Red Cross was further crippled by the ban imposed by the newly independent Government of Equatorial Guinea, first in January 1969, and again in March of the same year during the crisis which ensured between Equatorial Guinea and Spain. France also was of assistance with regards to relief which it unambiguously sent to Biafra through Gabon and Ivory Coast. The OAU in a mere *usus loquendi* had declared that the war was an African affair, but like a physician who cannot heal himself, sat and looked on as the war raged. On its on part, the United States having through the "State Department clarifications asserted that it continues to recognize the Federal Military Government as the only government in Nigeria," started sending cash and relief in millions of dollars to Lagos.[71] Nevertheless, the war ended in 1970 in favour of the Federal Government after a cease-fire. Whether or not the Biafrans would have won the war had the Federal troops not gotten military aids from Britain and the communist countries is a question beyond imagination, and therefore, not within the scope of this book.

The above was by no means a detailed account of the Nigeria-Biafra Civil war. This was a mere adumbration, to help in shedding some light (no matter how minimal) on the resultant effects of military intervention in politics. The presence of military administration is still

current and thriving in Nigeria today. With the exception of 1978 –
1979 when an attempt was made to return power to the people by
means of the ballot box, Nigeria has been ruled by one military regime
after another – frequent overthrow of government from one to the
other - since 1966 when the first coup took place, as mentioned above.
Sometimes the military does well, sometimes it doesn't. For instance,
the Buhari/Idiagbon Regime which flushed out Shehu Shagari's civilian
administration in 1984 was really determined to wipe out bribery and
corruption in that country through its policy called WAI (War-Against-
Indiscipline). No sooner had the policy gathered momentum than his
regime got toppled by a new regime - Babangida's administration. Since
after the first coup till today, military administration has changed
hands so frequently that sometimes one forgets which regime took over
from whom, when and what circumstance precipitated the overthrow.
More often than not, the reason is: "to eradicate corruption." It is quite
an enigma that, when the same Muhammadu Buhari returned to power
in 2015, he became one of the most corrupt presidents Nigeria had
ever known. For example, his kinsmen, the Fulani herdsmen terrorists
and Boko Haram terrorist organization have kidnapped, raped, and
killed thousands of civilians, mostly Christians, in Nigeria. But,
Muhammadu Buhari, who was once thought to be an honest, frugal,
and disciplined retired army General, would turn a blind eye to the
corruption, mayhem, and disasters occurring in Nigeria, particularly
if the perpetrators pitched camp with him.

While eradication of corruption may not always be the reason for
military intervention in some other African nations, a closer analysis of
the pattern seems to converge on the social and political conditions of a
particular society at any given time. As noted above, what prompted the
first military intervention in Nigerian politics was socio-political. The
riot was a social problem which was in turn caused by a political factor
and the end result was a military takeover. The most general reason
for military takeover used to be in pretence of defending the original
constitution. The frequency of the takeover has worn away such excuses
as it has been replaced with another such as to stamp-out corruption or
to remove an unsatisfactory leader. Those excuses can be used to fool

some of the people sometime. But it becomes frivolous if they try to use it to fool all the people all the time. Therefore in some cases they cite the reasons to be economic (not political) such as unemployment which was the motivating factor in the overthrow of President Fulbert of Congo - Brazzaville, in 1963.

However, what reason could the military have given for intervening as much as five times in Dahomey in 1969? They could claim it to be economic. Then what could be its reason in the overthrow and murder of President Silvanus Olympic of Togo in 1963? Perhaps that was a mere reproduction of the unrest following the Second World War.

The African soldiers who engaged in the war may have come home ready to flex their muscles in order to exhibit their newly-acquired military tactics. This could also be the principal reason behind Idi Amin's seizure of power after his experience in the military tussle with the Mau Mau in Kenya.

The psychological impact of the Second World War (and the subsequent wars such as the Congo war, etc.) could also have played an important role with regards to military presence in African political arena in the 1960s. From the look of it, a passive observer may be tempted to rashly conclude that military despotism has taken place only in the African continent. A closer study of world politics would reveal otherwise. From the time of the First World War to 1965, as many as thirty nations of the world had had some sort of military intervention in domestic politics. With this it may be argued that the army's intervention in politics is in essence a way of defending their profession. An army is defined as highly organized, highly disciplined, and acts with the expediency of *deus ex machina*. An army confronts any existing problem without delay. Its modus operandi is: Act now, question later. With esprit de corps as part of the military training and understanding, the army, working together, cannot sit around and watch while things go awry in their country. Thus, a good soldier takes up the challenge – to defend his nation against internal anomalies as he would external forces. The army therefore, sees intervention as an integral part of their duty; it is a necessary evil; it is a *sine qua non*.

In Ghana though, Colonel I. K. Acheampong's military overthrow of Dr. Kofi Busia's administration on January 13, 1972 was without much justification. The only apparent problem was with the economy. But it should be borne in mind that economic problem is more or less a natural phenomenon which may occur at one time or another, even in developed nations. As such, it should not be a sufficient reason to warrant a military comeback.

A few months previously, General Afrifa had peacefully handed over to Busia's democratically elected government asserting with confidence: "Now that our rifles are down, they are down for ever." With this statement, Afrifa (whose regime ousted Nkrumah) hoped his to be the only military intervention in Ghanaian politics.

But no sooner had Afrifa handed over to Busia than Busia being overthrown albeit the fact that Busia's administration already showed some characteristics of quality governance. Not only was it elected by a peaceful democratic process, his administration showed some good credentials for agricultural development as an effective tool to revamping the economy. A similar thing happened in Imo state of Nigeria, where a duly elected Governor, Mr Emeka Ihedioha, was removed from office by Nigeria's Supreme Court, and replaced with Senator Hope Uzodimma. The former belonged to a different political party (PDP), while the latter belonged to the same party as Nigeria's President, Muhammadu Buhari. Despite the fact that Emeka Ihedioha won the governorship election by landslide, and was already making some improvements in revamping the state's economy, he was removed, perhaps for partisan reasons. The Nigerian Supreme Court's blatant involvement in partisan politics on January, 14, 2020, and Acheampong's military intervention in Ghana's civil polity in 1972, for no credibly justifiable cause are clear indications that most African Supreme Courts and military are desirous to seize power, just at the whims and caprices of the Court and/or the army, with little or no justification for doing so.

At this point, a curious mind may have to ask: is the army capable of toppling a legitimate government without the power of the gun? That question triggers another: If the army of advanced countries, with all the ammunitions and/or military weaponry and military technologies at their spell could control their desire to involve in politics, why can't African soldiers do likewise? Or, could the interference be seen as a meal ticket to achieve wealth and fame?

The last question is in consonant with the observation made by Professor S. E. Finer that "military initiatives in politics are most often the product of a low level of political culture in circumstances where there has been virtually inevitable economic disappointment, compounded by financial mismanagement."[72] Various individuals may have various other answers. But, whatever their answers to these questions, military intervention in African politics should not be expected to last forever.

As society changes, so should the role of the military. As the mass of people become more and more educated, they know their rights, participate more in politics and become increasingly aware that the duty of the military reposes on defending the nation against external invasion, not on intervening in minor domestic squabbles (unless such a domestic problem is such that could threaten the existence of the state or country). Nor is the duty of the military in nation leadership, as the case may be. Their leadership and trophies should be in battlefields not on the altars of domestic politics. Major General Colin Luther Powell with his military might marched to the Gulf war and brought home to America the trophy of victory. Neither he nor any other military commander thought of flexing their military muscle in national politics.

Any wise military official desirous of joining a political bandwagon, should first keep his gun aside, take off his military uniform, then put on a political uniform and get ready for political challenges and competitions. Lt. Col. Oliver North (another US military Officer) only got involved in national politics after leaving the military; and so did Colin Powell among many others. One thing is clear here, the person or persons getting involved in politics did so after leaving the military, not while in the military as is the case in most African and other Third World nations.

Military intervention in African politics could be perceived as one of the major reasons for the failure of civil democratic polity as well as infrastructural underdevelopment in those nations. While it could be argued that the politicians are not better than the military, and vice-versa, the politicians in their effort to get re-elected, could be motivated to serve the interest of the people no matter how small. Conversely, the military, not vying for any electoral post might not be inclined to do the domestic chores such as re-building roads and infrastructures, etc. Also, the politicians may be adept in governmental accountability while the military may either not have such skill or may not want to justify its actions or inactions.

In this modern time and age, there really shouldn't be any reason for such unwelcome military intervention. Although I do not condone violence and riots, those should not be good-enough reason for military intervention. Political violence and riots happen all the time in Britain - Ireland and Scotland. The Royal Army has not yet overthrown the system. Neither should it suffice to claim the eradication of corruption as a reason for intervention.

Also, the military may have some handicaps in terms of inadequate personnel. This shortcoming they try to solve in some peculiar ways. One thing peculiar with African-style military leadership is relying heavily on the available permanent civil service. This was initially practiced in Ghana during the regime of Kotoka, and in 1972 by Colonel Acheampong. It is also still used by the current administration of J. J. Rawlins of Ghana and in practice in Nigeria. Perhaps this is not by choice but out of necessity.

It should be mentioned perhaps a thousand times that military intervention in politics has a great negative effect on a nation's image in international relations. Potential international investors would be very hesitant to invest in a country with frequent, turbulent change in government. Besides, military intervention forestalls political and economic developments.

It should be mentioned here, perhaps in passing, that the oddity of military politics is the habit of stopping whatever policy the previous administration initiated. In other words, the military is always in the habit of not completing programs or policies initiated by their predecessors. They either completely scrap the policies or programs and start all over, or totally abandon the policies of their predecessors. This is a waste of time, effort, talent, and money. A rolling stone gathers no moss. Our nations could achieve substantial economic growth, if new regimes continue policies, programs, or developmental projects from wherever previous regimes stopped. Such continuity will assure realistic and effective results.

In conclusion, military intervention in civil polity hinders political and economic growth and is loaded with lackadaisical activities and/or behaviors that encumber social advancement. Such must stop. Civilians should be allowed to manage their affairs in civil ways without military interruptions. If they make mistakes, they learn from such and make adjustments as they go along. That is the name of the game of politics. Should the military always whip out their guns to quell every political riot and usurp power to take control of every situation, then civility would be pathetically reduced and relegated to a precarious state of barbarity.

CHAPTER SEVEN

Renaissance of Democratic Polity

Political and civil society must normally devise new strategies for empowering themselves to monitor and control military and intelligence systems if new democracies are to be consolidated.[73]

In my humble opinion, democracy is the hope of a confused world. Having been globally engaged in totalitarian warfare in order to preserve this political philosophy as a way of life, we are not being consistent if we either restrict the development of democratic institutions or limit the enjoyment of the fruit of democracy to a few, regionally. In the interest of world peace, democracy is indivisible; one-half of the world cannot be democratic and the other half undemocratic, otherwise we are sowing the seeds of future war for, as Tacitus said, "A desire to resist oppression is implanted in the nature of man."   -Nnamdi Azikiwe

"Herbert Macaulay has left us a great legacy - the struggle for the attainment of social equality, economic security, religious tolerance and political freedom in our life-time. It is our duty to hold aloft this touch of democracy so that our posterity shall be free. It is an obligation for us to prevent repetition of the fatal mistake of living in servitude and in want even in the midst of plenty."[74]

Herbert Macaulay died in 1946. It is hard to believe that his dream of a democratic Africa in general and Nigeria in particular is still unrealizable more than fifty years later. It is equally hard to believe that it is now almost forty years since most of African nations gained their political independence, yet most of these nations still do have political tepidity at best and political mediocrity at worst. It could be stated that, perhaps, most of the ex-colonies are yet unsure of the system of polity to adopt. On one hand, Democracy is identifiable with imperialism, hence most metropolitan nations where democracy is operational were at one time or another associated with imperialism. This could explain why some of the newly emerged nations subscribed to socialism at the onset, after the attainment of independence. For example, Ghana under Nkrumah, and Guinea under Sekou Touré. The then leaders of these nations, among others, might have denounced democracy, thinking: how democratic were the (metropolitan) governments whose missions were identified with imperialism and exploitation. Two instances that call to mind here were Fidel Castro's Cuba, which was forced to turn communist following the antagonistic discord with the imperialist United States, and Jamaica, which is yet undecided whether to turn socialist or democratic. Perhaps, it would be better to turn Democratic-Socialism, like the Scandinavian nations, or Totalitarian-Capitalism, like the Nazi Germany. On the other hand, Totalitarian-Socialism and/or Communism have been associated with brute and failure.

Although they were previously not imperialistic, the savageness in policy and bankruptcy in economy with which communist China, Russia, Poland, Czechoslovakia and Nazi Germany were associated, was enough to make searchers of political identity to think twice, not only about the workability of communism but about the wisdom to incline in that direction. Feudalism has never been an option in any modern political arena. Perhaps, it has been viewed as a medieval political ideology and, as such, people look down on it, and no one attempts to embrace it.

Of all political systems, both mentioned and unmentioned, democracy is still the best. In my opinion, any other attempt at any other system is not only a waste of time but a delusion indeed. Hence democracy has proven to be the most if not the only workable political apparatus, our leaders should work hard at it and make it work within our nations. There is no other way out: If we cannot beat the system (democracy), we have to follow the system. There are no two ways about it. We should STOP deluding ourselves: Military politics or Militarism, Kleptocracy, Praetorianism, Totalitarianism,

Socialism, Communism, Thuggeeism, Anti-Semitism, Racialism, Tribalism, Imperialism, Colonialism, Feudalism and so on down the line are nothing but vanity and witch-hunting. History has proven that none of the aforementioned is workable; as a matter of fact, they only come back to hunt the person or body of persons, nation or body of nations that tend to practice them. This being the fact, shouldn't our leaders (or ulers) learn from history, and succumb to the only workable and prosperous alternative: Democracy?

For socio-political tranquillity and economic steadfastness, democracy should be introduced, or reintroduced as the case may be. It has to be fairly practiced and nurtured until it permeates our system, like second-nature. In the absence of this, we are wasting our time. One must bear in mind that there are no beds of roses without thorns. Although democracy is the best alternative, it does not come too easily. A lot of sacrifices must be made, the most important of which is: Dedication to honesty.

By this, pursuers of democracy must be committed to: Not rigging elections, or getting involved in any political shenanigans, gerrymandering, or any other electioneering malpractices. The populace must learn not to give or accept bribe (to or from) any unscrupulous political elements, or their thugs, or their stooges. One should always bear in mind that what is at stake is not just the future of the individual, but the future of the entire nation and its inhabitants. Thus: What Shalt it profit a man, to accept bribes of any sort and jeopardize the politico-economic development of his own nation?

The self-deification and financial aggrandizement which could emanate from such frivolous acts as in accepting bribes only lasts momentarily. In essence, by accepting bribes, one has accepted to sell ones birthright for a mere 'token pot of porridge, which one eats only once, and, it's gone. A case that calls to mind here was Shehu Shagari's election to the presidency in Nigeria's second attempt at democratic polity for which election was held in July of 1979.

Alhaji Shehu Shagari was "elected" for two consecutive terms as the President of the Federal Republic. In my opinion, the (first) election was fairer than the (second), or his "re-election". Even at that, the first election was not without blemish. For example, the Presidential candidate of the UPN (Unity Party of Nigeria), Chief Obafemi Awolowo on August 19, 1979, filed a petition against the declaration of Alhaji Shehu Shagari as President by FEDECO (the Federal Electoral Commission). "Chief Awolowo contended that Alhaji Shagari was not duly elected by a majority of lawful votes because he had not satisfied Section 34A sub-section (i)(c)(ii) of Electoral Decree 1977 and Section 7 of the Electoral (Amendment) Decree 1978.

He claimed that the election of Alhaji Shagari was invalid...A voter, Chief (Dr.) Olaogun Adeoye also filed a petition against the declaration of Shagari as President. In it, Chief Adeoye claimed that Alhaji Shagari was not qualified to be elected by reason of corrupt practices and non-compliance with the electoral decree."[75] A three-man tribunal sat, to look into the petitions. It rejected the petitions and refused to provide five classified documents "vital" to the petition. The request was turned down by the chairman of the tribunal, Mr. Justice B. O. Kazeem, on the grounds that "the contents of the documents would be injurious to public interest if produced."[76] Awolowo went to the Supreme Court. Among other things, he pointed out that the Tribunal erred in refusing to provide the vital documents needed to buttress issues in the petition. He also indicated that the Tribunal mis-directed itself when it took the total votes cast for Shagari in Kano State to be 243,423 instead of 203,460.5. Then, he cited that the Tribunal failed to properly interpret section 34A sub-section (I)(c) (ii) of the Electoral Decree 1977, as amended; etc., etc.

After all said and done, on September 19, 1979, the Supreme Court, presided over by the new Chief Justice of the Federation, Mr. Justice Atanda Fatayi-Williams convened. In the final analysis, the Court rendered its verdict: Shehu Shagari became the President.

During the first four years of his administration, things had gotten so bad that many citizens were literally eating off of dumps and dustbins, while at the same time some State governors were wasting money. For example Melford Okilo (of Rivers State) wasted a stupendous amount of money dumping sands into the Ocean in a futile (unwise) effort to reclaim land from the sea. On the same footing, while people were starving and couldn't afford a decent square meal a day, people of Umaru Dike's ilk were hoarding millions of tons of rice, beans, fertilizer, etc., (during Shagari's administration).

With the forgoing and much more, it is doubtful that any human being in his right-thinking mind would re-elect such a regime for a comeback to power. Nevertheless, that's what happened. In the subsequent election that took place in 1983, "ballot papers...intended for the election...were alleged to be in the hands of unauthorized persons in large number."[77] Bribery occurred, overtly and covertly. The election was massively rigged and the same administration was "re-elected".

During the second term in office, things went from bad to worse and from worse to worst: day-by-day. To save the nation, the military regime of Buhari/Idiagbon) usurped power and flushed out the so-called politicians for they knew not what they were doing. Ghana too attempted to revert (from militarism) to civil electoral polity. To make it happen, a general election was conducted on August 29, 1969. Five political parties (such as the Progressive Party (PP) led by Dr. Kofi A.. Busia, the National Alliance of Liberals (NAL) led by K. A. Gbedemah, the All People's Republican Party (APRP) led by Mr. Patrick Quidoo, the People's Action Party (PAP) led by Mr. Imoru Ayaraa, and the United Nationalist Party (UNP) led by Mr. Joe Appiah, including some other independent candidates, such that about 480 candidates) contested. The transfer of power from military to-civilian rule was so systematically and carefully prepared for that the election which was held was "conducted more fairly than any in tropical Africa since independence."[78] About 16,000 soldiers and police stood-guard to ensure a conducive atmosphere for free and peaceful election. Voters' turnout was enormous.

About 2.5 million voters registered for the election versus 1,459,743 and 2,098,651 in 1965 and 1960 respectively. The Progressive Party led by K. A.. Busia came first, capturing about 9,000 votes, winning all the seats in Ashanti, Brong-Ahafo and the Central Regions. The Party also won many seats in the Eastern and Western Regions. The National Alliance of Liberals led by K. A. Gbedemah secured about 8,000 votes, winning almost all the seats in the Volta Region. This being the case, Dr. Kofi Busia's Progressive Party, which won the election, was seen as being more successful in popularity than Nkrumah's CPP ever was. However, by 1971, Busia's administration started having economic problems. Austerity measure was introduced; importation of cars and television sets were banned. In addition, the currency got devalued by 48.3 per cent. The stringent economic condition awakened certain social vices such as corruption, prostitution, depredation, etc. But, no matter how economically bad Busia's administration may have become, in my opinion, it was still far better than Nkrumah's despotic government. For one thing, while Busia never attempted to proscribe the existence of other political parties, it was the first move made by Nkrumah. Also, while Nkrumah headed towards Despotism, Busia's was within the mainframe of Democracy.

Regardless, things went awry anyway. The economic and social conditions deteriorated a little further. At that juncture, the military led by Colonel Ignatius Acheampong came in, and flushed out Busia's government by means of coup. Be that as it may, military intervention in civil polity though welcome in some instances where elected officials tend to become despotic, as happened in Obete's Uganda and as should have occurred in Touré's Guinea, such intervention should only be for a limited period of time, say, a few months. Just to get things back on track. It becomes a scornful aberration when it lingers from months to years, ad infinitum.

In instances where unpopular governments gain control of power by illegitimate means such as by rigging of elections, the knucklehead electorates who allow themselves to be bribed, and who particularly indulge in rigging of elections (be it at the grassroots level or at the Federal or National Electoral College level), or those who indulge in any aspect of electioneering malpractice no matter in what iota, are the ones to blame not only for military comebacks but for the socio-political ills as well as other developmental backwardness of the nations involved. If the electorates could be honest and dedicated to change, elections may never be rigged. If dully elected officials make mistakes, they have four years within which to correct their errors and prove their administrative competence, otherwise, get flushed out either by impeachment or through the ballot box.

Politically speaking, nations ought to be allowed to make their political mistakes, learn from such errors, make adjustments, move-on from there and grow into a political adulthood. Most advanced nations made the same or similar mistakes, learned from such and made necessary amends. What politically kills-a nation is not making political mistakes but languishing in such mistakes. Another thing that kills a nation is not making any political and economic growth at all. Such either kills a nation politically, or submerges it and keeps it in a state of incunabula for a long time, if not for ever.

Thus, although rigging of elections is quite prevalent in the Third World nations, such is still not completely out of fashion in some of the so-called developed nations. Sporadically, electioneering malpractice rears its ugly head even in the United States of America, the fatherland of democracy. For instance, although the scrutiny has of yet not been finalized, the election of Xavier Suarez to Miami's mayoral seat in November 1997 is still under investigation following reports of massive absentee ballot fraud. Equally, in the electoral system of the United States of America of yesteryears, electioneering malpractice was not unheard of. Back then, "the Electoral College was an unreliable device. Through its malfunctioning, and the further unrepresentativeness of the House of Representatives, Jackson had been cheated of the Presidency in 1825. He had secured more popular votes than John Quincy Adams: both he and the American public had been thwarted. In consequence he had proposed to introduce a more democratic system of presidential election, but Congress had undemocratically refused to put the matter to the test of a constitutional amendment.

"However, neither the Electoral College nor Congress was able long to withstand the general will of the American people. In 1832 they placed Jackson in power, beyond quibble."[79] Two things of great import happened here. For one thing Jackson who was defrauded did not resort to thuggeeism, victimization, looting and killing in a way to show his anger. He rather channelled his energy toward devising a workable presidential electioneering apparatus. Also, he knew that the American people had spoken (through the ballot box), and that the people were with him (through their votes). He, therefore, was patient: knowing that *vox populi, vox Dei* (the voice of people, is the voice of God). His patience paid off. It was only a question of time. Then, the Congress learned that when the people speak, Congress listens. Secondly, the government learned not to force an unpopular government against the will of the people: when once public agitation is detected, the government succumbs to the will of the people for the most part to avoid major problems from occurring.

This is the way responsible governments develop. It does not come from thin air nor does it propagate in a vacuum. It is tamed, moulded, nurtured and grown before it blossoms into "pure" or "absolute" representative democracy.

Before this happens, three sacrifices must be made:

1. The citizens/electorates must be honest and candid about not rigging elections.
2. The military must stay out of politics (unless it is absolutely necessary, in which case its interference should be minimal and temporary). This would allow the people to make their mistakes and learn their lessons.
3. Finally, any defeated party (or contestant) should wisely and respectfully yield the ground to the chosen (duly-elected) one.

In politics there is no loser; only scholars. A party or person that is not elected, wisely studies what it did wrong, improves itself especially its policies and wisely presents itself again in subsequent election(s). Such wisdom and candour in accepting "defeat" and managing self for better result could save our nations a lot of social ills. Probably, the party could prepare itself well enough that it could catch the interest of the masses and get elected. For instance, in the United States of

America, the Democratic Party had not been elected since after Jimmy Carter. But the party never gave up hope, nor did it resort to any wrong doing that could tarnish its image. Rather, like any other wise party should, it kept studying what improvements should be made. Thus, in spite of George Bush's Republican Party's favourable activities in the Gulf war, the American people decided (through their electoral votes) that they should give Bill Clinton's Democratic Party a chance. The outgoing George Bush's (Republican) administration did not rig the election. Nor did it resort to repression, oppression, suppression, proscription and/or censorship in order to influence the outcome of the electoral result or to retain the presidency at all cost, as is usually the case in most Third World nations.

Much in the same vein, Margaret Thatcher did not impede John Majors from taking over from her when her administration became unpopular and John Majors became chosen (by the people, through the ballot box) to displace the Iron Lady (Mrs. Thatcher). Nor did John Majors hinder the newly elected administration of Tony Blair. It is mind boggling that Third World Nations in general and African nations in particular (especially West Africa, per se) copied almost all aspects of British and American lifestyle except: Humility. Our leaders should be humble in accepting defeated elections; in accepting their faults; in accepting to serve their people selflessly and in a dedicated fashion. If the whites in South Africa were able to accept defeat, and peacefully gave way to Nelson Mandela (a black leader in the aftermath of apartheid, the first in the history of the racialist country), why couldn't our politicians learn such humbleness of heart, accept political defeat when it comes their way and make adjustments accordingly? To prepare for free and fair democratic elections, political parties populated with (moderately) decent and honest members are required.

Political Parties

A nation can operate under one of three forms of political party systems. The one is single or one party system. The other is dual party system. And the third is a multi-party system. It is wrong though, to assume that every political system must have political parties. Militaristic polity does not necessarily use political parties, yet it is considered a form of political system. This being the case, it should be acknowledged that some political systems do not require, and do not necessarily utilize political parties. Thus, a distinction must be made between political systems and political parties.

While the former is the form of governance or an approach through which a nation rules its citizens and controls its socio-political activities, the latter is a mechanism or a vehicle or an apparatus with which to actualize the socio-political activities in a more organized fashion Parties are usually formed to compete for elections both at local and national levels. Sometimes, when a party wins, it may tend to subjugate, oppress, suppress, repress or even completely eliminate opposition parties. For example, such was done in Ghana under Nkrumah, Uganda under Obete and Guinea under Sekou Touré. Where such is the case, the State could be said to operate a mono or single party system.

In the event that a party loses, it could be the one to be eliminated at most or be driven underground at least. Perhaps that explains why most Third World politicians resort to any sort of sham practices in their efforts to "win" elections. In some political systems there may not be a complete victory by any one of the competing parties. When this happens, the wining parties may strike a balance among themselves or form a coalition.

In some other political systems, the parties, the executives and the military officers do share their powers with many other political forces. This has partly been applied in Nigeria, when Military administrations tend to work with (elected or) appointed civilians as state governors and local government chairpersons.

Totalitarian Parties

The Communist Party of the defunct Soviet Union could be seen as a perfect example of a totalitarian party. A totalitarian party is the be all and end all; the alpha and omega. It could make or break a man in any state where it operates, and to some extent, even beyond. In the Soviet experience, the party was so powerful that, even "extremely popular generals, such as Zhukov, feared as possible Napoleon Bonaparte, were relegated to obscurity, soon after the end of World War II. Also, many of the most popular leaders of the party itself were slaughtered by Stalin in the Great Purge of 1937-1938."[80]

In fact, in any state where it operates, no one can win popularity without the approval of the party. The party also discourages criticisms and does not hesitate to destroy potential opponents and/or rivals, whether real or perceived. As was the case in the Soviet Union, the totalitarian party monopolized all political, social, economic, industrial, technological and governmental/state apparatuses, Using collectivization of agriculture, the party owns the country's system of agriculture; thereby controlling what was produced and how much. Even schools and the modes of teaching were under the spell of the party. Thus, it produced, and educated its soldiers, cosmonauts, factory managers, scientists, politicians, industrialists, police officers, and managers of all other aspects of human endeavours.

The flow and management of information, in and out of the country, were also controlled by the party. This way, it controlled the content and the extent of circulation of political information. In other words, through its propaganda apparatus, the party decided what it wanted the citizens to hear about, and what it didn't want the people to know about.

Dictatorial Parties

A dictatorial party is one which tends to maintain absolute power and unlimited authority over the state, the government and the people. In some instances, as was the case with Benito Mussolini's Italian Fascist

Party, the dictatorial party only maintained partial control over the society. In this case, the church, the monarchy, the armed forces and big businesses, somewhat, maintained their autonomy. In some other instances, as was the case with both the Soviet and Nazi parties, the control was, more or less, all inclusive. A dictator is, more or less, a god to be feared rather than respected. Hitler, Idi Amin, Stalin, Mussolini and, to some extent Khrushchev, created much trepidation within their societies, and could almost, always do whatever they wanted at whatever whim or caprice they chose.

Nevertheless, the removal of Khrushchev from power and also the 1943 eventual removal of Mussolini, by the united force of the King, the police and the army, is an indication that a dictator could only last in power if the party and other socio-political forces accommodate the dictatorship. It is self-evident that most dictators know this. That could explain why some dictators, like Obete in Uganda, Nkrumah in Ghana, Bourguiba in Tunisia, Sekou Touré in Guinea, among others, first and foremost ban the existence of other parties in order to procure their positions against rivalries, then they convert their parties to personal instruments which could be used at the whims and caprices of the leader.

A distinction must be made here between dictatorial parties and dictators. While the former deals with the organization or the governmental apparatus, the latter has to do with the person managing that apparatus. For example, while the Soviet Communist Party was a dictatorial party, Mikhail Gorbachev was not a dictatorial leader. Conversely, even though Ben Bella of Algeria was a dictator, his party (FLN) was not. Perhaps, this accounts for why he was overthrown in 1965, because his party (members) did not support his dictatorial principles.

Dictatorial parties and dictatorial leaders have one thing in common: they hate criticism, and they outlaw opposition. Nkrumah outlawed all competing political parties, and so did Obete and Touré. In the defunct Soviet Union, no one could dream of establishing any other party besides the already existing dictatorial party. Any political opposition is considered a treasonable felony, perhaps, punishable by death. Infallibility and authoritarianism accentuate the tenet of dictatorship. They cannot be criticized and they cannot be opposed. In Fidel Castro's Cuba, you have the freedom of speech until you speak against the Government.

Oligarchical Parties

Oligarchical government is one in which the supreme power is placed on the hands of a few exclusive class of people and/or institutions. Oligarchical party is one that, directly or indirectly, maintains supreme control (not absolute control) of the political activities in a nation.

A good example of an oligarchical party is the *Partido Revolucionario Institucional* (Revolutionary Party) of Mexico which has ruled the country since 1929. The party shares control of the government with a few other institutions such as the executive, the church, the trade unions, and the armed forces. The control of the party is centralized in the hands of the President. And the President, being the leader of the party, controls the whole governmental system.

Although it does not outlaw the existence of other parties, they can function as long as their doing so does not threaten either the existence of the oligarchical party, or its ability to maintain its leadership position. In other words, other parties can exist under the shadow of the Big Party. In the Mexican situation, for example, other parties are allowed to exist, but they are not allowed to win many offices. Parties can be denied access to the ballot, in an effort to frustrate them from winning many elections. One outstanding difference between Oligarchical and dictatorial parties is that the one (to some extent) tolerates the existence of other political parties, while the other does not.

The PRI also allows the existence of competing interest group organizations which though are autonomous and could retain their individual identities, are affiliates of the party.

Strong Parties

A strong party is usually democratic both in outlook and in principle. It is called a strong party because of its ability to capture the mass appeal or the interest of the majority for an extended period of time. A good example of a strong party is the Indian Congress Party (the former Indian National Congress under Gandhi). The party has been able to dominate other parties in elections, not through repression, oppression, or suppression of other potentially competitive political parties. Rather, it has been able to maintain its hold of the people's heart by doing things the Democratic way. Since 1947, the party has been popular for its policy in always seeking to expand opportunities for employment, economic development and social reform.

The party also is able to win the hearts of the people for psychological reasons. For instance, it has always been perceived and respected as the party of Gandhi, the party of Nehru, and the party which won them national political independence.

Also, politically, the party has till date won its popularity for being able to suppress Communist threat. Economically, it is believed to be dedicated to rapid development and it delivers measurable results. In my humble opinion, this sort of party is what we should pray and hope for.

In conclusion, having studied some aspects of political parties, good citizens of our nations should be able to decide what sort of governance they would like to live under. Should it be Totalitarian, Dictatorial, Oligarchic, or Democratic?

In my opinion, no person in his/her right mind would shun Democracy after seeing the weighty flaws in which the other systems operate. There is no doubt that Democracy is the only progressive system of polity.

To bring it about, the people must be determined to divest themselves of any spirit of greed or parsimoniousness or avariciousness or any other desire bearing the emblem of corruption. During elections and at all other occasions, always pray that you be not led into the temptation of accepting bribes and thereby jeopardize the chances of actualizing a functional democracy. Resist bribes and save your nations from political and economic difficulties. Extricate yourselves from desiring to eat today and die tomorrow. For this matter, always remember that the worst thing you could do to yourself and to your nation is to succumb to the temptation of accepting bribe today and, directly or indirectly, plunge your nation into political and economic hardship tomorrow.

CHAPTER EIGHT

Black Man an Accomplice in Defrauding His Own Nation

Black Power is a doctrine about black people, for black people, preached by black people. I am putting it to my black brothers and sisters that the color of our skins is the most fundamental thing about us. I could have chosen to talk about people of the same island, or the same religion, or the same class - but instead I have chosen skin color as essentially the most binding factor in our world.

In so doing, I am not saying that is the way things ought to be. I am simply recognizing the real world – that is the way things are. Under different circumstances, it would have been nice to be colour blind, to choose my friends solely because their social interests coincided with mine - but no conscious black man can allow himself such luxuries in the contemporary world.[81]   -Walter Rodney

Africa has withstood the test of time and space from the beginning of the world. The happenings in that continent will determine whether or not the continent and its peoples will exterminate with time.

Africa and its peoples are at a crossroad, where they must either mend their ways or face extinction from the face the earth. According to Okot p'Bitek, "the ancient prophets were, in fact, poets commenting on the social and political issues of their time. They were not engaged in some distant future, for no mortal can 'know' what he has not experienced. They sang of love and hate, expressed joys and sorrows, and shed bitter tears to wipe away corruption of power."[82] The contemporary African does not need to await resurrection of the prophets of old, to know his continent is tending towards extinction following the trend of things. Shall the African become the dinosaur of the next millennium? Our current actions and/or inactions, will determine what position Africa will take in the annals of history come the next sesquicentennial or so. Some egoistic nincompoops could utter, "one-hundred-and fifty years (or more) is too far out to worry about. By then, we are all gone anyway."

Well, such utterance is a mere balderdash. Did our ancestors think along that line (150 years ago), we would not be here today. Should the black man defraud his nation for his own selfish ends, and aid in extinguishing his posterity? What does it profit a man, to gain the whole world, deposit the proceeds in foreign bank accounts, and suffer the loss of his own nation?

The concomitant problems meted in Africa are man-made. They were not of divine origin. The panacea of the problems should also be man-made, not divine. We broke it. We should fix it. In other words, since all the problems that confront us today were our own creations, either by our own actions or inactions, we and only we can solve our problems, either by omissions or commissions. We have to undo what we have done wrong, and redo what we have done right.

It is our task to make joy out of living. It is our task to extend that joy to our children and their posterity from generation to generation. So that they too will have life even more abundantly. "One of the greatest social philosophers of all times realized this rendezvous with life, and he postulated that he came into this world...in order that his fellowman might have life more abundantly (St. John x. 10)."[83]

Should not the African procure the future of his continent and follow in the same footsteps to make the posterity of his stock to have life more abundantly? Does not the African know that by aiding and abetting in the defrauding of his nation, he is directly or indirectly aiding and abetting in the extermination of his continent and its peoples? Can he not resist such a temptation?

The spirit may be willing, but the flesh is weak. That is

understandable. That is the way of all flesh. Nevertheless, if people of European stock could pave the way and make it smooth for the coming of their posterity so they may have life more abundantly, the African should, and the African must do likewise.

For, to the children are the honor and the glory. We cannot, and should not take it away from them. Much like John the Baptist advocated to pave the way, and make it smooth for the coming of the mighty-one, we too should pave the politico-socio-economic way of our nations, and smoothen the condition of things therein, so that those coming after us may have life more abundantly.

For theirs are the power, and the kingdom. We cannot, and should not take it away from them. To do so would be to rob them of their honor and glory. Does not the African know that his continent is shaken to the foundation of its existence by the forces of envy, jealousy, greed, and evil? Does he not know that his stock might be exterminated as a race, unwept, unhonored, and unsung, just by his actions and inactions, deeds and misdeeds, omissions and commissions, in just a matter of time (be it one hundred or one thousand years from now)? Does he not know that the seeds we sow now are what we and our posterity will reap in due course?

By defrauding his nation and putting the proceeds in foreign bank accounts, the African is making things rough for his kind and conversely enriching life for the Anglo – Saxon stock and the like, wherever the proceeds are deposited.

In every human being, there is an acquisitive instinct compelling him to possess more and more wealth, ad infinitum, if given the chance to do so. It is the acquisitive instinct which propels a man to callousness and jealousy against his fellow man, if he fails to have as much as the other. It is also the acquisitive instinct that gave birth to greed; making us reap where we did not sow; making us defraud our nations.

Thomas Hobbes knew what he meant by asserting that man was wolf to man. In the nature of the trend toward acquisitions, man becomes a wolf. He tends to justify his actions on the ground that life is a struggle, wherein only the fittest will survive. "Thus if force...is used to attain this objective, militarism is glorified as a pruning hook...

Hence, even though evil means are used to attain a goal, the end is justified." Or so they think.

"This acquisitive instinct has been responsible for the revolutionary ideas of history. The man with the capital proceeds to amass more wealth."[84] Even when and where it means: Defrauding his own nation. It is time for the Africans to desist from tottering the economic pillars of their nations, infiltrating their societal galleries with calamities and stunting the political, and techno-industrial developments of their nations.

Grassroots Politics (Where to Begin)

To make democracy work in African societies, especially in those nations were it seems a near impossibility, the value of fair electioneering practices should be taught at the grassroots level. The lesson should be taught that when a government is no longer popular, the incumbent should yield to the duly elected-in-coming officials rather than reverting to subterfuge, gerrymandering, and rigging of elections. It should be learned that the only avenue to a tranquil, politically stable society can only be achieved through the ballot box.

People should learn that no corrupt administration endures forever. That of Idi Amin never did. Neither did that of Ferdinand Marcos of the Philippines. As the world turns, it brings about changes. As the world is not standing still, regimes must come and go. No administration (civil or military) can monopolize office for ever. Nor will the masses dance forever to the whims and caprices of any evil empire. Reforms are a continuous process in any given society. Sometimes they come through peaceful means; sometimes by violence. It depends on how the leaders control the masses at any given period. No person or group of persons in their right minds would prefer violent revolutions to peaceful ones.

However, as President John F. Kennedy said, "Those who make peaceful revolution impossible will make violent revolution inevitable." It is up to the leaders of any given nation to decide which path to reform they prefer their subjects to toe. It could be argued that the black man is so peace-loving that he may never resort to violent revolution in an attempt to liberate himself and/or his nation borrowing from the fact that the black man has gone through multitudinous devious acts since the beginning of time, and yet has not revolted to alter the course and change his plight.

Nevertheless, I surmise that the black man acts more out of cowardice than the love of peace. How can the African hope for peace when there is no equity and no justice? How can we hope for peace when the dreams, and the future, and the aspirations of our children and their posterity's are taken away by the few who pose to be our policy-makers? By those who pose to be our leaders? By those who believe that the resources our nations are endowed with are their personal birth-rights? By those who cannot countervail the forces of time nor could they render rectitude to our existence and our sufferings? By those who egoistically care about only themselves and their children, regarding us and our children as nonentities, whippersnappers, and amorphous masses? Should we exist like this for ever and not demand a change? There has not been anyone who loved peace more than Jesus, according to the scriptures. Yet, He became radical and revolutionary when He overturned the table of the money-changers, and demanded with impunity that the House be reserved as a House of prayer to His Father.

Much in the same way, we in the Third World should ask for peaceful transformation of the occurrences in our nations. Should it be far-fetched, we should radically and in a revolutionary form, "overturn the table" in order to bring about the needed change in our social, political and economic milieus. Thus, we should assert that our nations and the treasures therein are for us all, our children's and their posterity's. Should our governments pay no heed to our demand for change, we should radically and in a revolutionary form, effectuate the desired changes. He who has ears, let him hear!

Revolution is not necessarily militant. It could be peaceful. And, it could be violent. Either can occur at any given place and time depending on the given circumstance. Be that as it may, I advocate that it is only when the peaceful process to a revolutionary change is ignored that a radical, or violent, approach should be taken to bring about the desired effect.

This brings up the question of education, but not necessarily conventional education. The more subsumable education the masses have about the problems facing their nations, the better off they are in knowing whether such problems are being addressed with efficiency or with mediocrity. Education also, affords them the means through which to bring their national problems to the forefront of their governments' attention, confronting the latter in the most suitable manner. First, peacefully; but, if they are shunned and not listened to, then they should decide in what other language to address their problems before their leaders.

Education is a good vehicle for societal changes. When the mass of people get more educated, more urbanized, and more politically awakened, they place more pressure and more demand on their government to provide social amenities – better roads, more efficient hospitals, increased participation in issues affecting the people such as politics, etc. If these demands are not met in a satisfying way, displeasure and discontentment would ensue; this might lead to a rife of civil disobedience, violence, riots, criminality, and what have you. The upheaval could climax to there being a friction between the state and the populace. At this point, revolution is imminent - it could be by peaceful transformation, or violent means. A perfect example of this is the recent insurrection that took place in Ecuador. Effective January 8, 1997, Ecuadorians went on national strike and vowed to remain on such strike for as long as it would take to bring Abdala Bucaram's corrupt regime to its knees. The economy came to a near-collapse, but the people succeeded in removing him from office. In civilized nations, peaceful transformation is more often than not the preferred method, for the leaders and the subjects know that unrest is an impediment to progress. Unrest, therefore, is avoided by wise leaders.

The transformation becomes peaceful when the government listens to the need and/or demand of the people and effectuate the change in a timely fashion. It becomes a violent transformation if, on the other hand, the government paid no attention to the people's demand, and the change was nonetheless effectuated either by tottering the government, completely displacing it, or by merely forcing the government to bring about the desired change. In Nigeria, for example, people voted against President Goodluck Ebere Jonathan; in their desire for a change, they voted in Muhammadu Buhari. To their dismay, Buhari's regime became the worst nightmare Nigerians have ever witnessed since the inception of that country.

Nevertheless, making governments accountable is what is needed in Africa in particular and in the Third World nations in general; especially in countries where the natural resources and the wherewithal are available, but the masses are living in penury in the midst of such plenty whilst the privileged few (leaders) are enjoying the wealth of the nations. It is quite ignominious for developed nations to assume that "Latin Americans and other peoples of the Third World ...failed to achieve development and modernization... because they lacked... industriousness and... failed to see their own problems. In effect, the blame for poverty and powerlessness was placed squarely on the poor and powerless."[85]

For one thing, it is nothing less than ignorance and myopia for any person or body of persons, country or body of countries to assume so; whereupon, the backwardness which these nations entered into was created by the countries which made their industrial progress to a large extent out of those nations.

Additionally, one must bear in mind that the masses of those nations did not choose to be poor. Such fate, more often than not, is dished out to the populace by their leaders through the leaders' ineptitude and ineffectiveness in managing the natural resources of these countries. The fact that it happens in Latin America, Africa and other Third World nations does not mean the people are not industrious or that they lack a sense of vision. Nor does it mean the people lack the acumen to solve their problems. It simply means that they are unfortunate to have inept governments that solve no problems - nationally speaking. Such could be the plight of any nation and its citizens, given the same or similar circumstance.

However, although such is the case, the masses Do Not have to swallow such bitter pills till thy kingdom come. It is their inalienable human rights to not only change their destinies but that of their children and that of their nations at large, bringing positive results rather than extinguish the destinies of their nations in the gallery of development. Should our nations atrophy at the incunabula of development? Should our nations not join the theatre of adulthood in social, political, technological, economic and industrial developments? Must the African be encumbered by the ambiance of cowardice and thus be deterred from saving his nation from plummeting in fiasco?

In spite of all its affluence, the name 'Africa' has been reduced to a word of opprobrium. Africans must strive to efface this undue appellation. In my humble opinion, the one possible way this could be done is by restoring pride and dignity in our nations. However, because the battle is a formidable one, we must first instil confidence in ourselves, and thus be able to carry the task of rebuilding our nations. Without confidence, our efforts could become a nullity.

We have to have confidence and with comradeship stand to challenge the spirit of cowardice. Although the flesh is weak, we have to stand firm even unto death, to bring about the positive changes in our societies. Change is necessary. Change is vital. Change is inevitable; at all costs. "What is at stake is not the destiny of a single country but the...destiny of the African continent... and the fullest development of the many countries comprising the continent,"[86]

It is quite understandable that "amidst the concatenation of events in this world, man is at times faced with insurmountable obstacles. The odds seem to be against him. And it appears as if all is lost. To surrender would seem to be the easiest way out. It seems discreet to yield so as to gain a purpose - possibly, individual protection. But a careful analysis of the part played by great men and women of history shows that those who surrender usually do so either because they lack the will to fight to the end or because they are forced by circumstances.

There are in this life, circumstances which force a man with stout heart to play the role of a coward. There are circumstances also which force a weak man to play the role of a hero. Amidst these vicissitudes of life... the African must take courage...the African must shun cowardice.

Let him look at the facts of history nakedly. Let him believe that he will and there is no force to stop him from achieving.

'Be not afraid, it is I,' said Jesus.

Why did Jesus assure his disciples that he was present and that there was no need to be afraid? Because he knew that the failings of mankind made them to be victims of the inferiority complex. They are therefore afraid whenever any phenomenon baffles them.

This is exactly the position in Africa today. Many an African... have failed ...because of heartlessness. Africans are afraid because they do not believe. They...show...they are incapable of ruling. Africans are subject races because they prove what they are by how they live and by how they think.

Renascent African, be not afraid. Be faithful unto death, if even to die is to make it possible for others of your kind to live... Africans have flesh and bone and blood like the rest of creation. Africans think like all higher animals of creation, graced under the name of mankind.

Africans eat and sleep and live and die, like others. Yet they are woefully behind the rest of mankind, because they are afraid. Be not afraid. Discard your chains, for they are only figments of the imagination.

Look at the rest of mankind. See how they are...mentally emancipated from this doom of destiny. They are human like yourself. If they could, you could. And if they would, you must.

Be not afraid. Wake up and claim your heritage or be for ever destined to draw water, to hew stone, to carry bags of cocoa, to row surf boats, to dig ditches - yea, to be the scavenger of the other races, for ever.

Be not afraid. Go forth and claim your heritage and enjoy life more abundantly, like the rest of humanity, or forever hold your peace, for by your dereliction of duty and apathy, you prove your unworthiness to enjoy this glorious heritage of mankind."[87]

Oh! Africans, Must you wait till this life comes to pass? Must you stand and look while the goodies of life elude your sons and daughters? Demand change when you should. Bring about change when it is necessary. This could be the only way to make the African dream a reality; without which it could be said that you and your race have been condemned to eternal doom.

Oh! Africans, what other recourse do you have? What else could you do, to change the plight of your children and the African posterity? What joy is there in you, to envision your children lose their life, lose their future, lose their world, and lose their dream of a prosperous African continent? Should you be so myopic, cower and shy away while the future is wrung out of the hands of these innocent children, and their world is disrupt even before it begins?

The African must not standby and look-on. The African must do something. He must not be afraid. He must effectuate a positive change in his society. He must not tend to save his life to the detriment of the future of the continent, nor to the detriment of the existence of the continent, nor to the detriment of the world of the children of the continent thereof.

As Jesus gave his life so the world could be saved, we must make the same or similar sacrifice to save the future and the world of our children, and to save our continent and its peoples from extinction. With this in mind, we must relentlessly pursue autarky in all its ramifications – socially, politically, economically, industrially, scientifically, technologically, and so on and so forth. When we accomplish a stable socio-political economy we then can relax, join hands with the young and the old and enjoy a hula-hula dance, for a job well-done. Without the actualization of such fundamental elements of societal developments, we are deluding ourselves with nothing short of fiddledeedee and hopelessness. The African must bear in mind that if other nations achieved the heights of developments, the African could; the African should; and the African must. Nothing is stopping the African from such accomplishments. The African is the only one stopping the African.

PART II

The Path to
Economic Stability

CHAPTER NINE

Roots of Economic Instability

The attainment of political independence is not tantamount to economic independence. Africa is known to be the most economically backward of all continents of the world. Although there is no reason for it to be so, Africa's economic situation, more than ever before, is more and more in shambles. Obviously, the ugly economic situation is fundamentally rooted in the five centuries of exploitation by America and Europe. However, the question remains: what should be done to save the continent from slipping further into destitution?

First, the Africans must have confidence in themselves. Then, resist all temptations – physical pressure (financial urge) and psychological pressure (greed) in looting their own nations, directly or indirectly. Finally, the people should then build on what they have. We should stop fooling ourselves, and stop looking for help from abroad. Such help is not there. It does not come without serious consequences which might mean psychological, political, and economic thralldom.

We have to learn that there is no such thing as free-lunch. They all come with strings attached: to the benefit of the lender and to the woes of the recipients. Until we realize that only the black man can rebuild his nation, we are still in slavery, at least psychologically. As Heaven helps only those who help themselves, we cannot expect anyone else to save us from the economic squalor we plunged ourselves into. Unless we do it, no one else will do it for us.

Except in the mid-nineteen-seventies when some major African nations, like Nigeria – deriving from the oil-boom, enjoyed affluent economic stability, African nations have been in continuous economic disarray since after independence. Although the fathers of African nationalism may have known that the actualization of political independence did not and does not necessarily mean economic independence, not much has been done to win economic independence as much as was done toward political emancipation.

A number of factors could be held accountable for this. One, which is very paramount is military intervention which started occurring, almost immediately or, soon after the winning of political independence as was evidenced in the Congo (Zaire), Ghana, Nigeria, to mention but a few.

Perhaps, economic independence could have been pursued with the same vigour and conclusiveness as was the political one. Although the military had often times seized power to hinder corruption, it is not certain whether military rule is indeed better than civilian rule. For one thing, while the civilian regime is more amenable and its deeds and misdeeds could be brought to question, who could question the activities of the man in uniform behind the barrel of the gun; except, perhaps, his comrades?

Be that as it may, the fathers of our political independence should have been given the time to correct their mistakes. Flushing them out has not, till today, solved our economic problems. To a marginal extent, perhaps, economic stability could have been won had the successors geared their efforts to that front. General Joseph Mobutu of Zaire tried in that direction, and so did General Afrifa's regime in Ghana and, before his assassination, Mutala Muhammed of Nigeria. Thus, it could be argued that it is not really what sort of governance that matters but who is governing and under what policies.

General J. J. Rawlins of Ghana has, heretofore, saved his nation from economic fiasco. Nevertheless, constant (rapid) change in government via coups and counter-coups is not economically healthy for any nation. It does not take a genius to understand that political/governmental instability scares off foreign investors. Also, it encourages even indigenous investors to take their money to other nations where stability is more or less assured. Another seed which germinates economic problems in our midst is the fact that the cash crops (cocoa, groundnuts, coffee, etc.) produced by African farmers are still sold, not to Africans but, to the metropolitan west. In the same vein, the mineral resources, petroleum, Aluminum, Tin, Bauxite, Copper, Diamond, Iron, etc., mined in Africa are still being supplied to the developed nations as raw materials, rather than being used in developing African industries. Finally, the devaluation of our national currencies has done more harm than good to the economic strength of our nations. About ten years ago, or thereabouts, the Cedi, Dalashi, Birr, Naira, Leone, etc., were all strong. For example, then, Naira was about two times stronger than the US Dollar. But due to the devaluation which followed, Naira is now eighty-five times weaker than the Dollar. Our currencies have continually been reduced to ghost-money. Money, money everywhere but not strong enough to buy anything with. Our governments should endeavour to stop the devaluation of our currencies. It is not healthy for national economic growth nor does it foster economic stability.

The Need for Economic Stability

Let's do it for ourselves.

Let's do it for our children.

Let's do it for our children's children, and their posterity.

And, let's do it for our good-hearted nationalists, who Fought so gallantly to liberate Africa and the Negroid Diaspora from political bondage; so when they look Down from heaven, they would smile on us with joy; that We finished the task they started, and not let it lapse. In this, I pray.

Throughout Africa, except to some extent South Africa, no nation enjoys the relative economic self-sufficiency available in the developed nations although the resources abound for economic opulence. The abundant national resources if properly harnessed and directed could enable most if not all individual African nations to achieve economic autarky equivalent in proportion to what is obtainable in most of the advanced nations, say Canada and Sweden, not to talk of the United States.

Unfortunately after having rid our nations of colonial rule, we have let the fortitude to self-realization in other areas particularly in economic aspect to lax. One should realize that political independence is more or less a nullity without economic independence. Without economic independence our nations could become a fertile ground for, and fall prey to, the forces of economic imperialism (i.e., neo-colonialism).

If such happens, thenceforth, we are deluding ourselves thinking we've achieved our national independence whereas ipso facto, we merely substituted one form of colonialism for another. It, therefore, suffices to say that the actualization of independence in all ramifications of that term, particularly in economic spectrum, is a sine qua non.

Our Head of States should make it imperative and should officiate, in economic developments. Economic developments, besides national security, should be given the topmost priority in national budgets. The Heads of States, by the virtue of their offices, could "re-animate" the economy by building industries and by making small business loans available (through the banks). With time, this will drive the economy forward, which in turn would restore our national image, reinstall individual dignity and, satisfaction would emerge from the progressive standard of living.

Diversification should be accepted as a shibboleth for agriculture development. The development of it should be geared more toward feeding the nation. In the same vein, the products manufactured by our industries should first be applied in nation-building after which the remnant could spill overseas by way of exportation; for, beautification should begin at home.

Without solid economic development, we are merely deluding ourselves in thinking of national development. It is impracticable to dream of national development without first having a strong economic-base. For this matter, the governments should develop and utilize the available national resources (skill as well as material) and use them to produce a strong, healthy and balanced economy. Without solid economy, our nations will continue to lose skilled human-resources as those who find the way would be obliged by necessity to take their skills elsewhere.

CHAPTER TEN

Exodus

The brain-drain of a nation is the one way of keeping that nation perpetually poor and in economically depressed state. Economic hardship and its causal effects of political instability have induced many intellectuals to migrate to the West, East, and the Far East. Many of these intellectuals have resided in their "new found land" for ten to twenty years and some will stay for the rest of their productive lives, working and helping in the development of their abode. These young men and women who are schooled and educated in Western political ideas, may not feel comfortable going back to their countries of origin, after having been away for so long coupled with the ever-messy economic statuses prevalent in their mother-nations. Their being away, prevents them from directly involving in the day-to-day politics of the people, and impedes them from impacting their ideas and knowledge of the western political system, in the absence of any other viable alternative, in their community. Thus, their skills and academic intelligence are more or less not used to effectuate the desired economic and political changes in their respective mother-lands.

There are millions of skilled and semi-skilled Africans from all walks of life-Archaeology, Engineering, medicine, pharmacy, economics, commerce and industry, to mention but a few - who are now living permanently in Europe, Asia, America, etc. because of the economic opulence and political stability found in these areas; forgetting that those economically and politically stable nations where comfort and peace of mind could be gotten did not emerge over night to be so. Neither were those nations born that way. Those were made to be so by men and women who put forth their best to such effect. In West Africa, for example Nigeria, the United States of America is referred to as "God's own country". This to me is a misnomer. If Africa is the birthplace of man, God's own country ought to be found in Africa. The United States is referred thus because of its political stableness, the economic opulence it enjoys, and the abundance of other socio-economic opportunities available to the citizenry. It took more than two hundred years of dedication and relentlessness in its pursuit of economic and political stability to get America where it now is in the arena of the world's political economy.

God, being ubiquitous, can find Himself a home in more than one country. All we need to do is: rebuild our individual nations, to achieve the same degree of political and economic might (if not better) as did the Americans. Any nation can build or rebuild itself if it maintains a consistent focus toward economic growth and political stability. For example, in the sixties Japanese products were not the best and its economy did not make it into the world map. But today, it is the world's leader in economic growth.

Thanks to its relentless pursuit of excellence. China, the most populous country of the world, is gearing toward the same direction of economic solidarity. Someday, theirs could be called "God's own country", while we standby and look. If the Japanese and the Chinese could do it, so can the Africans. And so should they. However, I am afraid any serious economic stability could be achieved in African nations without first putting a stop to the transference of the natural resources in general, and human resources in particular. The importance of human resources can never be over emphasized. In his day, Adam Smith (in The Wealth of Nations) was able to recognize that "the skill, dexterity and knowledge of a nation's people is the most powerful engine to its economic growth".

Great nations of the world could not have attained such statuses, had their intellectuals migrated and spent most of their productive lives elsewhere. This is precisely what is happening in the African nations in particular, and the Third world nations in general. When the intellectuals leave, they do so with their knowledge and skills. Whatever country they settle in, is who benefits such a pool of human resources. These skilled men and women add to the already existing "most powerful engine" of the host nation as they, through their labor, join in bolstering the economic growth of the said nation. The United States of America was not stupid when it started its "Visa-by-lotto" program, targeting the rich and/or skilled, intelligent men and Women from various countries of the world. Such a group of people would bring in their talents and skills, and thus, contribute toward the economic growth of the host country.

In Africa people "live under the tyranny of the tropics, paying heavy toll every moment for the barest right of existence (Rabindranath Tagore)."[88] Drought is the middle name of most African nations especially the land-locked areas. Torrential rain is not uncommon within the coastal regions. When it shines, it burns. When it rains, it pours, like from deep abyss of hell. The climate is excessively harsh. This renders the land barren or unarable, and uncultivable as the top soil gets washed away and/or made sandy. Erosion is another subset of the problems caused by torrential rain; making it difficult for fruitful and progressive agriculture. The "typical tropical weather, never moderate, always extreme. Too much rain, or too little. Too much heat. These brute physical facts of life in developing countries are...primary causes of poverty. If you open any decent atlas at those nice, blotchy maps on temperature, rainfall, soils and vegetation, notice that the problem of underdevelopment appears to be confined to the tropics, between about thirty degrees north and south of the equator.. The developing countries get more than their fair share of rainfall, and of drought."[89] How long shall the problems last?

Perhaps for ever, if nothing is done about them now. While one cannot do anything to offset the course of nature, one can delimit its effects. To make agriculture more fruitful, the government and the private sector should invest more in irrigation, flood control, erosion control, and mechanized agriculture. Water supply should be made available at every nook and cranny of the nation so that farmers could irrigate, and water their farms. While this may not completely cure the problem of drought, it suffices to say, it will go a long way to mitigate it because, "given enough fertilizer and water, year-round sunshine can create an extraordinary agricultural potential, allowing as much as three crops a year."[90] Modern agricultural equipment such as fertilizers, tractors etc., could therefore be used in curbing the harsh effects of mother-nature. Also relentless effort should be made by the government and individuals to protect and preserve top-soils from being stripped of manure by hash climatic conditions. This could be done by leaving no land exposed. All exposed lands should be covered with grass, plants and vegetation. On the same token, all roads should be paved and tarred. The foregoing will to a great extent curtail erosion.

Moreover, good paved roads will foster transportation, communication, and commerce. In many West African countries roads are unpaved and full of potholes. In some instances the roads are completely impassable making it excessively uncomfortable, if not impossible, for easy movement and trade. Thus bad roads hinder transportation, mobility, commerce, and encumber agricultural growth. Altogether, the effect is debilitating to the economy. Bad economy produces excessive hardship which in turn forces people to peregrinate.

Another hazard to agricultural growth is the flourishing of insects. In the words of Abbe Dubois, an eighteenth-century French traveller, here, "every kind of irritating, destructive and abominable insect swarms and multiplies in a manner that is both surprising Land amusing."[91] These pests include houseflies, sand flies, tsetse flies, black flies, tiger-mosquitoes that carry microbes, fungi and parasites. They attack and debilitate livestock and could sometimes be the epicentre for diseases which might bring "concrete economic costs to the individual, his family and his country. It reduces a man's productivity as surely as hunger does."[92] There is also the question of caterpillars eating up the crops. Such havoc as these could be impeded with the use of pesticides.

The government should encourage research in the manufacture of pesticides and should make them sufficiently available for use in private and public farms. Reduction of these pests would enhance and/ or increase food production which will in turn reduce misery and make life worth its while. Land-tenor system is another factor militating against productive agriculture. Lands are individually owned in bits and pieces by members of the community. In this case, the government should encourage buying over the lands and converting the same into public farm-land. The foregoing would improve agriculture, food production, the standard of living, and make life a lot more comfortable. When people are more comfortable and happy, they put in their best and become more productive in the community. This helps economic growth and makes it less desirable to migrate.

It has been mentioned, perhaps to the point of ad nauseam, that when people migrate from one place to another, they take their talent with them. Economic hardship within the continent of Africa has induced the intellectual apparatus of our nations to migrate, in search of a greener pasture commensurate to their educational attainment. In most African Airports, one cannot fail to notice the volume of people fleeing their native countries on daily bases. Running away, will not solve the problem, it would rather exacerbate it.

It is human nature to seek the easy way out. To seek comfort and maximize his happiness whenever and wherever possible. This could explain why people move from economically bankrupt nations to more affluent ones in search of opportunities to maximize their joy. Nonetheless, one should not forget that those nations where peace of mind and comfort could be found were made so by human effort. The same degree of peace, comfort, and happiness could be achieved in our nations and communities.

However, "everybody is more inclined to neglect the duty which he expects another to fulfill".[93] This is where and why the governments should take the initiative to create jobs and other social opportunities, this would serve as a base upon which the individuals could stand to develop their skills and talents. With the achievement of relative degree of comfort, the need to migrate would be curtailed. Only when this happens will the "exodus" stop. And only when such movement stops shall the economy start to thrive, without which political stability would be, but a dream. Working consistently toward the same goal will in the end produce the desired result(s). Much may not be accomplished by individual effort. Although collective effort is required in order to effectuate a noticeable change, the first stride will have to be taken, if not by the government, by the individual; for, the government starts with the individual. This way, "the political needs of society become individual needs and aspirations, their satisfaction promotes business and the commonwealth."[94] With the collective effort of the individuals, the society is built. When the society is cohesive they work toward the same goal for the commonweal. This promotes the economy which in turn paves the way for a stable government. For example, Americans are the most patriotic citizens than any country one can think of. Regardless of their racial diversities, they work together to make theirs the number one country of the world - "God's own country" - if you will. With the help of the government and the law, everybody works toward making the society a comfortable place –economically and politically. This, perhaps explains why Americans don't like to travel abroad. It is not that they are afraid to travel. If and when they travel, they don't like to stay too long. Not that they don't have the money to spend. The fact is that they have more comfort and opportunities available in their country than they could find elsewhere. Thus, to travel and stay abroad is a discomfort to the American. The opposite is the case to the African who, in spite of all the negative treatments he receives through racism, contents himself with staying abroad, to the detriment of developing his own nation. The Koreans and the Japanese perhaps have realized this and have embarked on solidifying their economy thereby, stifling the need to migrate. Wherefore should there be any migration in this case, it is for other reasons but economic.

On the other hand, in our own nations, economic imbalance is the primary inducement for migration. Capital flight is on the increase, unemployment is the order of the day, and so is underemployment. Stagflation reaches higher heights on monthly bases, and the currency values of our nations are on continuous decline. With these recurring problems, economic crisis would always be on the increase and things will always grow worse, unless the circle is broken - the sooner the better.

CHAPTER ELEVEN

The Concept of Nationalism

The term nationalism can make or break a nation, depending on what, and how the nationals of a given nation conceive it to be. The term "Nationalism" is a derivative of the word Nation. The term Nation, can be defined in one of two ways.

(1) In a narrow scope, it can mean a stable community of people speaking one language, have one distinctive culture, share same or similar economic life, have a common historical origin, and found within a territory (e.g., a people, a race or tribe).

(2) In a wider definition, the term applies to the people within a terrain or confines, united under one government (e.g. a country or a state - Ghana, Togo, etc.).

The term Nationalism, on the other hand, means: (1) devotion to one's nation (i.e. patriotism); or (2) the belief or credo that national interests are more important in one's life than personal life or international considerations (i.e., internationalism).

One of the principal elements of the problems in contemporary Africa is the lack of distinction between "Nation" and "Nationalism". For the most part, the concept of nationhood (tribe or race) has been the banner of our principle and the tenet upon which our actions revolve. Thus, an African would specifically prefer to deal with his people (tribe) and feels he has actuated nationalism, than he would feel, if he did something in general for his country.

The misconception of the term "nationalism" is not found only amongst Africans; even in Europe, the concept has oft times been misused, at least in conduct. For instance, had the Yugoslavians not identified specifically with their respective tribes or ethnic groups, as opposed to nationalism, disintegration would not have been possible, nor would it have been necessary. With this in mind, it could be said that nationalism, in most cases, is wrongly used on a micro level to apply only to one's race or tribe; whereas, the applicability of the concept should be macro, that is, going beyond the race/tribe to encompass the nation under one government. Thus, in the Yugoslavian spectrum, had they not atomized the spirit of nationalism, had they a sense of political statehood, national consciousness, and that paramount identification with the nation-state, disintegration could not have been in the offing, and it would have been unnecessary. Another classic example is the British Isles - England, Scotland, and Ireland. Their preference in identifying with their own, rather than identify with the macro element of the political statehood of Great Britain, has been the epicenter of discord in that country. Thus, it would be incorrect to identify African nationals as the only ones who interpret nationalism in a narrow fashion.

Nevertheless, nationalism, in its truest defined form, does not exist in Africa nor does it exist anywhere in the world, for that matter. An American Negro would identify with his race first before taking the next step towards identifying with the political statehood. And so do whites. Regardless that the Americans are still the most patriotic citizens in the world, racial identification still comes uppermost. As a matter of fact, it is the core of Racialism. Throughout the African continent, the only homogeneous national group are the Somalis.

The lack of macro-identification (true nationalism) with the nation-state has had some serious consequences in Africa's political and economic development. This is because the myopic definition given to the concept has created the spirit of separatism, sectionalism, favoritism, and nepotism.

Thus, a particular ethnic group who happens to have the privilege to be in power tends to bring the chicken to roost in his 'part of the nation' - race or tribe. No wonder the vehement struggle to be in control of the power apparatus. Not necessarily to have the privilege to do things for one's nation in general, but to do things for one's race or tribe in particular. For example, "most Nigerians have come to believe that unless their 'own men' are in government they are unable to secure those socio-economic amenities that are disbursed by the government."[95] This purports to say, if their "own men" (i.e. people from their tribe) are not (leaders) in government, their part of the nation may be unable to secure the essential amenities in terms of development.

Make no mistake about it, blood is thicker than water. That which binds a race (or a tribe) together is thicker, and therefore more valuable to them, than that which holds them within the nation-state. This is why ethnicity, by and large, is still the highest and, perhaps, the most impenetrable form of identity.

In conclusion, the term 'Nationalism' ought to be a concept connoting patriotism, with deep-felt identification with the nation-state. However, at the national level, that is not what is practiced in most, if not all, African nations and, perhaps, other Third World nations. Knowingly or unknowingly, this has exacerbated underdevelopment in our nations socially, politically and economically, as leaders may tend to develop more of their individual ethnic regions than elsewhere.

This is not the way things ought to be. But that is the way they are. And that is the essential reason why we need to mentally, psychologically, socially and nationalistic ally redefine (our view of) the concept: Nationalism.

The Need Redefine Nationalism

We should regroup, re-evaluate and redefine nationalism, making it extend beyond the microcosm of our tribe or race; thereby giving it the right true definition that it deserves. Furthermore, the term should be given a deep-rooted, profound interpretation with national consciousness - patriotism. We should cling to a definition not myopically focused on the tribe alone but that which transcends the tribe or race and encompasses the entire nation-state. Thus, it suffices to say, we should conceive "Nationalism" as that aggregate of group identity which passionately binds diverse individuals into a people. The nation thus becomes the highest affiliation and obligation of the individual, and it is in terms of the national "we-group" that personal identity is formed; that is to say, instead of identifying oneself with one's race or tribe or group, one should go beyond that and identify oneself with the nation-state: thus, rather than say, I am a Quebecer, or a Manitoban etc., one should say, "I am a Canadian".[96] It is only when this sort of identity is formed that nation-building can be done effectively, and efficiently for the benefit of the current and future generations of that nation.

In this regard, if the Americans can get along to build their nations, so can we. At this point, one may succinctly argue that American nationalism (in its true form), perhaps, stems from its "melting pot" heritage, and therefore, they do not have any other choice but to get along; thereby, believing that the historical circumstance which brought the Americans together was quite different from ours.

That while historically, they individually or collectively sailed forth to the "New found land" and settled therein of their own accord, we, on the other hand, were so lumped together by no choice of ours but by the circumstance of our colonial parentage.

Though this is factual, it suffices to point out, arguendo, that neither of the historical legacies is changeable. In other words, neither can the contemporary Americans, nor the contemporary Africans, nor anyone for that matter, possibly change the history of our legacies. This is an irrevocable fact and that has been proven, and will continue to be proven; and nothing can be done about it. As such, we have no choice but to get along.

And this can only begin when, and only when, we re-examine and redefine the concept of nationalism in a new light with an altruistic purpose. Without this approach, our countries or nationals will go in shambles.

I may not be a prophet, nor a Messiah, nor do I profess to have all the answers to our problems, but truly, truly, I say to you, unless we change our attitude toward each other, unless we change our image towards our nations, unless we change our perception of nationalism, the possibility of achieving a politically, economically, and technologically empowered new continent geo-physically, would be equivalent to 'a camel passing through the eye of a needle.'

To accept the new concept, one has to first exorcise one's mind of the old concept. A deep, profound mental and psychological surgery should be done, without which one is only deluding oneself. For a second step toward "mental emancipation, the apostle or disciple of the New Africa must hurdle over barriers of race or tribe. One must be willing to be called names and to suffer persecution, so that truth may be allowed to flourish on the earth.

In other words, the disciple must forsake mother and father and relatives and friends, and even homes, so as to leave Nazareth for Jerusalem and proclaim the truth from Mount Olives, if even the goal is Calvary."[97] The road to socio-political stability and economic opulence is thorny. It is filled with a lot of self-sacrifices. It is filled with denying oneself of the necessary niceties and giving same to ones nation at a macro, not micro, level.

Those privileged to be at the helm of administration, both at the national and local levels, should realize that they were appointed to show the light, so the less-privileged masses may see the way. The case of Major Anthony Ochefu, the onetime military Governor of Anambra State of Nigeria, comes to mind. He originated from another state, and was appointed the governor of Anambra state. He was upright and steadfast in executing his task in that region. Even though it wasn't his state of origin, he treated it as if it were. Although I was yet a kid then, I still remember what good people spoke of him throughout that state. However, as rumor had it, some disgruntled elements who perhaps failed to receive expected, but undue, favours saw to it that he got removed and got retired "with immediate effect". Everyone that I knew went to bed early that day for they could not withstand the chill which beclouded them upon hearing it on the News. As a matter of

Ejike R. Egwuekwe

fact, some were so much filled with pangs that they turned off the TV, also "with immediate effect".

Aside from Anthony Ochefu, there have been some other good administrators like Commodore Ndubuisi Kalu and Brigadier Ike Nwachukwu, whose eminence in leadership (even in regions not their states of origins) has made me believe that, even though we are still far from it, some patriots have grasped the true concept of nationalism, and are already putting their knowledge of it to work.

Thus, the one-thousand-mile journey has already started with a stride; we shall not be left behind. We must all follow. And realize that it is our collective responsibility to develop (any and) all parts of our nations, whether we originate from there or not.

IRREDENTISM

The term Irredentism was an 1878 coinage following the formation of an Italian political party whose main purpose was to join Italy (by whatever means possible) the adjacent regions populated largely by people who spoke the Italian language but were under other governments.

Geopolitically, the term Irredentism can be used to explain the internal aggression of one region against another for the main purpose of expanding its border or territory. In this school of thought, the term can be stretched to encompass disputes between ethnic, racial, religious and linguistic groups, as long as the primary intent (or the primary purpose) of the aggression is to incorporate the 'prey' into the aggressor's territorial control.

The interest groups doing the aggression could vary. It could be social, political, economic, or even religious groups. For example, a person or a group of religious fanatics struggling to take over another group's congregation could be seen as an irredentist (group). A point must be made clear here: What characterizes Irredentism?

Three qualities characterize Irredentism: (Unification, Reunification, and Expansion):

(1) It must be a struggle for unification. For example, the Hausa speaking peoples of the Central Sudan are found from the Niger-Benue junction (including Northern Nigeria, Northern Ghana and Chad) all the way to the desert South of Agades. Although they are not of the same race, they speak the Hausa language. For this reason, if any of the group intends to aggress against another such group for the purpose of unification, it is an act of Irredentism. The centripetal force of attraction here is Language. But the purpose of the aggression is unification. Bear in mind, the only thing these people have in common is language.

(2) It could be called Irredentism also, if one or more groups vie for reunification after being torn apart by either war or any other circumstance beyond their control. For example, during the colonial era, Cameroon was split in three. One portion was a French-holding. One was a German-holding; while the other was English-holding. After World War II, the German were driven out and its portion got sheared between the French and the British. However, the British annexed its shear to Nigeria for easy administration.

Nevertheless, the (British) portion got reunified with the other parts before the attainment of political independence. Although there was no aggression involved in that process of reunification, it still could be called irredentism as long as it involved one of the characteristics, in this case, reunification; especially if a political movement was entered into for that purpose, as was the case in Cameroon. Irredentism, therefore, does not necessarily have to be aggressive.

(3) For that matter, although all irredentist acts are not always aggressive, all aggression for the purpose of either unification, reunification, or extension, is irredentist. For example, around 1845, the United States fought Mexico, conquered, and annexed the areas around Texas, California, etc., territorial

expansion was its motive. Also, when one village within a tribe or race skirmishes with another village or town for the purpose of expanding the other's territory or boundary, it is an act of irredentism.

The boundary disputes which often occur around Eket, Ikot-Ekpene, Ikom, Ngwa, Ndi-akata (in Southern Nigeria), is another case in point. The main motive here is expansion of territory or border. Therefore, it is irredentism.

CHAPTER TWELVE

Literacy (The Key to Economic and Social Mobility)

> Education is not only the key to personal enrichment.
> In the Third World context, it should be the central
> mechanism by which entire villages and urban
> communities learn to develop themselves, their
> productive potential, and their resources.[98]

The inferiority complex entrenched in the African was infused through the umbilical-cord linking Africa to its colonial parentage. Serious surgery by way of mass literacy must be done, to change the situation. What is needed is some mental surgery.

What is needed is some mental emancipation. Without this, the complex is so deeply entrenched, 'am afraid not even the River Jordan can cleanse it. "The African has not been in a state of incunabula throughout history. There is no scientific proof to sustain the idea of superiority or inferiority of any race, physically or mentally. For the African to cultivate an inferiority complex that he is inferior to other races is to sign the death warrant of Africans. Emancipation is therefore essential.

Let the African know that he had a glorious past and that he has a glorious future. Teach the African to know his capabilities and his role in the scheme of things. Let the African realize that Burns was right when he said, 'A man is a man...'

Rid the African of all complexes which would retard his growth towards manhood on the theater of nations. Let him follow Socrates: *Gnothi seauton* (Know thyself), and like a sleeping giant let him awake and harness his power for his own good and for the good of mankind. This will create mental emancipation, for mental slavery is worse than physical slavery."[99] Literacy is the only avenue to reach mental emancipation.

Unfortunately, the level of illiteracy is so atrociously high that something needs to be done about it with unrestricted immediacy. Although the level varies from one African nation to the other, illiteracy is still found in alarming proportion throughout the length and breadth of the continent. Of all the problems inundating Africa, illiteracy should be the easiest to solve, and therefore, does not have any reason to remain a problem even as we march into the Twenty-first century.

The future of the continent is in the hands of the African children, and the future of the African children is in the hands of the governments. For this reason, I unequivocally assert: It is the duty of our governments to provide a meaningful literacy mechanism through which our children and their posterity would see the light at the tunnel of their journey in life. May the governments alleviate the already compounded burden on the African populace.

A number of measures could be taken to eradicate illiteracy at best, or reduce it to the barest possible minimum, at least. In most African nations, people pay their way, from kindergarten to university level in quest of education. In a poverty-stricken continent, this is not only had on the people, but almost always impossible for an individual to foot. Because of this, the governments should provide tuition-free education from Primary school to Secondary school levels. Or, just at the Primary school level, at least. This could alleviate some burden, even at a small scale, off the people. The relatives of the scholar can take it from there.

In the event that the bill of "free-education" is not possible for the government to handle, would it be too much to ask that our governments supply the needed books to our children so we can take care of the tuition and fees? I don't think so. Elementary education (at least) should not be a privilege. It should be a birth-right to African children. Because the children are the future of the continent, it is our collective responsibility to educate, and show them the way. Without good education, African children may not be able to compete in the ever-changing world. We have seen how tough the world is. Let's imagine how tough it would be on these children, to compete with the other educationally-conscious and serious-minded students of other continents like Asia, Europe and America, if they don't have adequate education to prepare them for tomorrow.

Furthermore, we have seen what ill fate visited our ancestors as they were cheated of the often mentioned mineral resources (which we know only happened, because our forefathers didn't know any better). On the same footing, have we forgotten that our ancestors were bamboozled into selling their children and relatives into slavery by the literate ones from the West? Now that we have tasted and seen that education is good, shouldn't we proffer to offer a good foundation of it to our children and the generation that comes after them?

A case that calls to mind at this point is Nigeria and some other West African countries where academic institutional strikes are a constant occurrence. Therein, many youths ranging from seven-year-olds to seventeen-year-olds, turn to street peddling. No schooling. No education. They embrace illiteracy, even in this Twenty-First century. If things are tough for even the most literate in these societies, how much tougher would things be with these future illiterates (if they continue their trade, without any formal education)? Wouldn't their plights be much worse than what we know today? Wouldn't a situation like that increase the number of urchins, and exacerbate hooliganism in our societies? If such wouldn't, nothing else would. However, rather than let situations of this magnitude deteriorate any further, governments should device means to make mass literacy an accessible phenomenon.

The Need for Technical Education

> It is worse than stupid to allow a people's education
> to be under the control of those who seek not the
> progress of the people but their use as means of making
> themselves rich and powerful... - W. E. B. Du Bois

It is an enigma that baffles understanding as to how come the African copied all aspects of Europeanization, save in areas of technological and industrial advancement. There is no doubt that "Africa is technologically the most backward of all three developing continents. Yet to compensate for the accidents of geography and geology she ought to be the most advanced."[100] One of the problems anchoring Africa's technological development is the imitative clerical-based system of education rampant in our nations. Such a system was devised during the colonial days to produce indigenous men and women who would do mostly clerical work for the colonial interest.

Now that colonialism has come and gone, we should restructure our academic apparatus, and lay more emphasis on technical-base system of education; to put our nations in motion to turn along with the world. Not that these institutions don't already exist in our nations, the number is not enough. For example, in West Africa, there are many Secondary schools, colleges of education, as well as universities whose curricula are still more focused on social sciences, languages, and the arts (i.e., clerical-base).

While a half loaf is better than none, what the African really needs is more of technical education which will in the end produce, not just technicians, but future scientists to man our mines, factories and corporations. Without this system of education being the most-favoured, it would be after the next creation of the world that Africa would be amongst the continents to put man on the moon.

Make no mistake about it, there are far more intellectuals in Africa than the world could ever know of. What needs be done to bring them to the surface is to reform the system in general and education in particular. This, in my opinion, will regenerate our technological malaise and backwardness.

One of the ways to ensure qualitative technical education is to encourage privatization of educational institutes at all levels. This will introduce the spirit of competition, and encourage efficiency and dedication. Also, privatization of education would eliminate any room for licentiousness, lousiness, or laziness on the parts of the scholars, teachers and proprietors, for they would know, winner takes all; and no one would like to be a loser. With this at the back of their minds, everyone would be dedicated to bringing their institution(s) up to par. Excellence, thus, becomes their hallmark.

This way, our societies could begin to actualize the technological and social progress that we lack. In the same school of thought as Nnamdi Azikiwe, I postulate "at the outset that scholarship is coterminous with social progress. It is the scholar who makes or unmakes society. He may not be appreciated by his generation, or even by generations after him. But time offers reward to scholars who lay foundations for the society of tomorrow, by immortalizing them in human history.

The African should go beyond the veneer of knowledge. Ability to quote Shakespeare or Byron or Chaucer does not indicate original scholarship. The capacity to know what is the periphrastic conjunction, or to solve the Pythagorean problem, or to understand the principles of heat, light and sound, or to translate Aramaic, or to know all the important dates of British history, does not indicate true academic scholarship. These are the superficialities of a decadent educational system. These do not make for a dynamic social order. They are by-products of the imitative complex which Gabriel Tarde expounds excellently in one of his books.

Originality is the essence of true scholarship. Creativity is the soul of the true scholar. Initiative, emulation and the urge to be intellectually honest are the earmarks of research and academic freedom. Heirs and heiresses of the New Africa must now consecrate themselves for scholarly research into all the aspects of world society in general and African society in particular.

Herodotus said that Africa ruled Egypt but that does not necessarily mean it is true. That Professor Bonehead taught that the African race have not shown any capacity for civilization, and therefore could not have ruled Egypt, except in the mythology of the Greeks, does not mean that this view need be accepted."[101] However, the only way to refute such derogatory statement is by embanking on the type of educational system that would put the African in direct competition (if not higher) with the rest of the world in areas of science and technology.

Most of our school laboratories for Physics, Chemistry and Biology are ill-equipped. If we could produce scholars who excel in these areas of sciences even after having studied in such scientifically bereft conditions, how much more brilliance could have exuberated from them had they had the opportunity to study in well-equipped, better-quality, and more sophisticated laboratories.

Knowing that solid scholastic aptitude is the only channel through which to efface such opprobrious assertions as Professor Herodotu's, our governments should owe it as a duty in equipping our scholars with the essential tools (i.e., fortification of laboratories etc.) and put our scholars *en route* to technological know-how. Only when this is done, at least at that level, may we begin to dream that our nations are on the way to technological development.

In conclusion, what the African needs is not more clerical-based education; but technologically-based or technically-based. Our governments could make this possible in many ways ranging from direct provision and/or equipment of our school laboratories to privatization of academic institutions at all levels thereby planting the spirit of competition and dedication to duty in technical academia.

Without solid technical and scientific institutions and the bright scholars they may produce, ours may never be able to compete with other continents, and may unfortunately continue to be seen as an opprobrium. Africa needs scholars. Creative scholars. Scholars who should emulate and not imitate. Scholars who eventually would lead our nations to the promised land of technological and industrial advancement thereby making Africa and its posterity to see the light at the end of the tunnel and acclaim that there is joy in scholarship. It is incumbent upon our governments to prepare the way and facilitate this eventuality. Well-to-do private citizens should have to help in whatever way possible to bring this to pass. They do not have to stand akimbo and look-on while our educational institutions go to ruins. Somebody has to revamp the system and provide the right tools

Thus, if the African is given the right tool and the right education, he has been given a place in the sun and a place to stand upon. Watch, he will move the world.

Industrialization: The Tool to Revamp the Economy

> In the field of science, change favors only the prepared mind. – Pasteur

Industrialization is the life-blood of the wealth of a growing nation. To achieve a solid economic base, African nations must have a far-sighted industrial plan or strategy. Without this, it might be difficult to achieve a consistent economic growth. To maintain a steady focus, we should always ask ourselves what type of industrial structure could be workable for the people; how can this be achieved, within what period of time could it produce the expected result, and how could the result impact the society; who benefits and to what extent?

When an industrial strategy has been adopted and the focus made, we should work toward that industrial structure within a projected time period, and stay right on that strategy, none-stop, till that goal is accomplished. There is nothing esoteric about industrialization. The French did it, the Americans did it; so did the Germans and the Japanese. Africans can do it too. But without such a strategy, 'am afraid, we may not go too far.

During the days of creation, God had put Adam into a slumber, whence he did not realize when a rib was taken from him. The African, perhaps, deriving from his direct Adam parentage has been in slumber right from the incunabula, at least for the most part. It has been mentioned in chapter two how we were robbed of our resources while in a sleepy-state. This time around, we are in a dormant state while the age of industrialization eludes us by. Of all developing continents, ours is the most backward, technologically, industrially, politically, economically, and otherwise.

Whatever may be the reason(s) for such backwardness, it is not a lack of intellectual apparatus. The fact that Ojukwu's Biafra was able to stay a three-year war with Igbo-made weapons (e.g., Ogbu-nigwe, Ojukwu-catapult, shore-battery, etc.) suffices to substantiate the African is equally talented with technological know-how, especially in times of necessity. Do we have to wait for necessity to knock on our doors, before we switch on the light of technology?

Two cases that call to mind at this point was in 1989 when I went to my village and chanced into two or three locally manufactured cars; and the case of Damian Anyanwu, a then seventeen year old student of Emmanuel High School, Owerri, who invented an air-plane and a Radio station right in his mother's hut. Unfortunately, the efforts of these geniuses (and others) were never investigated and sponsored. Such efforts did nothing but atrophied. Such should never have been the case. Such efforts should never have been wasted. They should have been effectively sponsored and utilized. In Nnewi, the ingenuity of the Igbos can be internationally reckoned with, as manifests in the products of Innoson Car manufacturing company.

Although necessity is the mother of invention, we do not have to wait for it to give birth naturally for it may never come to pass. We have to mobilize our resources, and put what we have to work. For example, some years after the war, the Nigerian government could have assembled all those local men and women (from the East) who invented the "Biafran ammunitions," subsidize their ingenuity, and have them developed.

All over Africa, there are men and women who have what skills it takes for technological development. The governments and well-to-do private citizens, should not close their eyes and turn the other way when it comes to financing such efforts. Such geniuses should be encouraged and their efforts should be sponsored and developed. This, in the long run could save tons of money in the importation of industrial machines.

Had this been in any of the metropolitan countries, I bet something good ought to have been done with such brains. How else does technological industrialization start? Definitely, not by importation, at least, not for the most part. Otherwise, how far could Japan have gone, had it imported all, or most, of its technology? For this, I surmise, unless we start investing in and supporting our indigenous scientists, we may not get too far in technological industrialization. And, we may keep lagging behind till the end of time. Up till this moment, backwardness in areas of industry and technology has had grave consequences in our socio-political-economy; consequence so detrimental that Africa is heretofore considered incapable of self-sustenance. Be that as it may, Africa's inability to maintain economic subsistence is the heir of its colonial parentage. It could be traced in that direction because, till this moment,

Africa is still highly dependent on world markets and is still highly involved in patterns of trade which are the product of the colonial past. Although this has often been complained about as the root of neo-colonialism, nothing has yet been done to change it.

And the West has retained it as one way of maintaining hegemony over Africa's economic development, though not by force but of necessity. It is quite acknowledgeable that most if not all the African countries are trying to build up their economies and to maximize domestic production of such basic items as textiles, cement, canned goods, beverages and other consumer soft goods, in order to save foreign exchange and to provide employment for domestic labour.

However, shall our technological growth stay at that elementary level? Must we not grow into the adulthood of technological development? Let the African pick on at least one element of industrial machine, and develop it to world renown-professionalism; much like the Swiss made a fame from watch-building. This is not impossible to come true in Africa. The talent is there, as was mentioned before. For example, watches were invented since the beginning of time, but there has not been a single African nation that manufactures a single watch. But, any watch and, in fact, any machinery, including motor vehicles, no matter how badly damaged, can be put back to effective use in Igboland of Nigeria. This means to say, there is brain power, not only over there, but in most parts of the African continent. What the people lack is support (i.e., governmental subsidy).

It is my suggestion that the government in conjunction with the private sector should device a strategy for industrial development. This could be done in many ways such as:

(1) The government can build, own and run all the industries (Communist method; though this is not the best approach, it is better than nothing).

(2) The government can build, own and run basic industries and allow private entrepreneurs in other areas (Socialist approach).

(3) The government and the private sector can jointly build industries.

(4) The government can make out, and guarantee business loans to serious-minded indigenous entrepreneurial industrialists; making sure such loans are repaid in due course, with equitable interest. More so, making sure such monies are used for the intended purpose (i.e., building of industries), this would, at least to some marginal extent, hinder unscrupulous persons from channeling the money to any other fraudulent effect.

(5) Or, the government can build the industries and lease them out to the private sector who would be paying an agreeable sum of revenue, periodically, to the government. This last approach, much like the first, is not the best for it could pave the way to quid pro quo, favoritism, nepotism, and mismanagement of resources: there is a propensity to lease or sell such industries at nominal fees to friends and/or relatives of the members of the government. However, much like in the first proposal, it is better than nothing, as the citizens could at least have jobs in their milieus.

A few years ago, the Nigerian government tried its best to have community banks built in every locale of Nigerian community. While this was a very good gesture in an effort to encourage and/or promote savings as well as provide jobs, it could have been better if industries (no matter how small) were built in all such localities instead of banks; banks however, could come afterwards. Thus, I postulate that the building of industries in every such locale, would go a long way in promoting the economy thereby raising the people's standard of living. The foregoing would trigger a chain reaction of socio-economic autarky within the community in particular and the nation in general. The effect of this could be well understood when analyzed from a critical standpoint. At a very elementary level, say industries were built in every community instead of banks. People working in the firms and industries would earn money to pay rents. The landlords/landladies could expend the money in local flea markets etc.

Directly or indirectly, this would positively trigger a chain reaction of economic buoyancy, sooner or later. It is at this secondary level that community banks ought to come into the picture, to hold the remnants of the proceeds generated via the local industries. It suffices to say that building community banks without first building industries is like going in an anti-clockwise direction. Members of the community (i.e., villagers) may not have money to save in such banks, if they are unemployed. In such a situation, even if deposits are made, withdrawals would follow soon after. This therefore defeats the purpose, and relegates the economy to the precarious status quo.

In view of this, it can never be overemphasized that industrialization is quintessential in the development of a nation. Without it, the functionality of the nation's socionomics would be a nullity at worst and bankrupt at best.

To save our nations from such a circle of doom, we need not just industries, but competitive industries that will, sooner or later, put our nations on the same plane of elevation as the so-called industrialized nations. To attain such a height, one must always bear in mind that, as George Strigler said, the competitive industry is not one for lazy or confused or inefficient men. Thus, it is one thing to strive and attain the desired height of industrialization, it is quite another, to strive and keep the industries up to par in efficiency. Without a candid consistency in pursuit of efficiency, the nation, in my opinion, is merely funambulating on the theatre of industrialization and may soon fall back to the status quo. In other words, if a nation succeeds in attaining its desired height in industrialization, the nation in question must couple such attainment with managerial and production efficiencies. Failure to do so could bring about a downfall which, perhaps, may relegate the said nation to its pre-industrial status, if not worse.

In the unfortunate event this happens, a bundle of problems could precipitate ranging from migration of the nation's best employees (to overseas), to dissipation of assets in terms of the investments made to attain the aforesaid industrial height. In view of this, it would be cheaper and wiser, to maintain efficiency at any cost and thereby prove that industrialization is a splendor.

Equally important is the fact that, in most African countries foreign corporations, rather than Africans, are the ones that control mining, manufacturing, and public utilities. This exacerbates capital flight. It makes me wonder: What happened to our indigenous engineers - civil, mechanical, metallurgical, etc.? Must we continue to give these contracts to those who fleece our nations, when we have our local sons and daughters who are equally capable of doing the job even at a substantially reduced pay?

By giving such contracts to foreign companies, the message we are sending to our children is that they are inferior to the metropolitan corporations. Thus, ingraining in them the white man's philosophy that blacks are inferior and therefore cannot function, while the contrary, indeed, is the case.

With this in mind, I hereby proclaim that, heretofore, nothing has stopped us from attaining technological and industrial heights, except ourselves. And if we continue to give these services to foreign corporations while our sons and daughters sit on and look, well, industrialization belongs to the nations of origin of those corporations, not to us for, it may never come our way.

How else can technological industrialization come to us, if not from within our midst? There is no other way, because industrialization is a technological apparatus of the people, in the people, for the people, by the people. It cannot be implanted. Nor can it be imported. Nor can it be transplanted. Any nation or body of nations hoping to buy all the needed technological machinery for its industrial development, is deluding itself and will wait a lifetime or until hell freezes over, yet, it may still never come.

If one travels to any of the technologically developed countries, sooner or later, one would acquaint oneself with Racialism and the fact that it has been often argued that the Negro race has not contributed to the development of the world and human race. This statement is inundated with falsity, as a keen examination of it could reveal otherwise. Nevertheless, it is an opprobrious assertion. We need to efface ourselves of it, and reclaim our dignity. The only thing to do is: Industrialization; technologically speaking.

Africa is the second largest continent. By this, it is a giant. A sleeping giant. Shall it stay asleep till the end of time? It is not for me to decide; for I know my answer. But it doesn't matter. And perhaps doesn't count. What matters and counts can be found at the hands of our leaders. Where they pilot the airplane is where it goes. They can pilot it to safety, or to crash; we and our nations are at their mercy. Thus, they have the yam and the knife, if they give us a piece, we may eat otherwise we have no choice but to starve.

It is really very saddening and very defacing that no African nation is among the "G-7" (or Group of 7 industrialized nations). It is now G-20; and Nigeria, which claims to be the giant of Africa, has not become a member of that group of Industrialized Nations; what an opprobrium. If it is not humiliating enough to stir the sleeping giant from its slumber, the giant should at least wake up for its children are starving. This being the case, our nations should incline toward industrialization, at least to create the needed jobs for the masses. This would create prosperity and reduce social vices that plague our nations.

Since the potentials are there in terms of resources, at least in human elements, nothing stops Nigeria from aspiring to become a part of the industrialized nations, and at least save its name from opprobrious negativism. Make no mistake about it: Nothing stops Nigeria from attaining industrialization even if it is only in the Agricultural sector. The resources are there. If China can achieve industrialization, and can feed its people, Africans also can. Africans also should, and must. The

African is industrious and entrepreneurial by nature. Since ages, the African had always struggled, against all odds, to keep body and soul together. The African has always been self-employed, and has almost always known how to take care of its own. This being the case, all he needs is a little space (governmental assistance), and he could move the world.

Governmental assistance does not necessarily have to come in direct financial grants or subsidies per se. It could come in terms of secured (with collateral) bank loans. Although it is true that oft times, loaned monies are used for other luxurious purposes other than for the originally intended effect, there are some good-willed individuals who are starved of credits and loans.

Granted that these well-intentioned men and women may not get the grants they deserve. Is it enough reason for their ideas to go to naught? If their ideas are unrecognized, and let to die, the error of such neglect has some deleterious effect on the growth of our nations' economy. A case in point here is the Awka people of North-Western Igbo land (in Nigeria) who were shrewd in blacksmith technology, arts, and sculptor. Because of lack of finance this area of knowledge has been let to decay. In most cases, the knowledge dies with the holder and does not get passed on. Two reasons account for this:

(1) because the genius was never encouraged/funded, he probably died poor (being unable to develop his skill to the fullest potential). For this reason, his offspringand/or relatives may not find it worthwhile to follow in the same direction, nor would they have the motivation/inclination to develop any other skill they may have.

(2) Closely related to the above factor is that most people pursue other ventures, particularly white-collar jobs (if they can find one) rather than develop their skills. Probably because the former accords him more dignified status than the latter. More so, he may have seen the impecuniosity which had befallen his relative (discoursed before), and therefore, may not want

a revisitation of that. In avoidance, thereof, he detours and/or circumvents the development of his skill.

In conclusion, industrialization is the life-blood of a nation. It is a sine qua non in nation-building. It is quintessential in socio-economic development. There are no two-ways about it. Governments and private citizens can, and should, team up to bring industrialization to bear in our milieus. When, and if, industrialization comes our way, we must strive to back it up with efficiency otherwise we would be only dancing on a tightrope in the industrial arena. No matter what it takes to attain the height of industrialization, it's worth it. In the same line of thought with George J. Stigler, we should relentlessly pursue industrialization; bearing in mind that it rewards both hard work and genius, and "it rewards on a fine and generous scale."

PART III

The Path to Administrative Accountability

CHAPTER THIRTEEN

Routes to Administrative Accountability

*Incrementalism
*Responsiveness *
*Competence
*Greed
*Accountability

For our nations to grow socially, politically, economically and industrially, administrative accountability (governmental and managerial) is of quintessential importance. The five spirits which could be modified in order to facilitate the state of development are: Incrementalism, Responsiveness, Competence, Greed, and Accountability. Such modification should be pursued and maintained. It is necessary to do so for a nation's development. It is a sine qua non. The five elements and their relative importance are individually addressed in this chapter.

Incrementalism

The term Incrementalism could be defined as continuous development from the foundation laid either by previous or current administration. The peculiarity that typifies most military administrations, especially in Africa, is to abandon old projects initiated by previous regimes. A good example of this was in Ghana, after the ousting of Nkrumah by General Afrifa's regime, everything that had anything to do with Nkrumah was scraped ranging from his ideology (Nkrumahism) to his economic principles to his application of socialism; even his disavowal of colonialism.

In Nigeria, when the civilian administration of Shagari took over from Obasanjo's military regime, it displaced Obasanjo's "Operation Feed the Nation" with what it called "Green Revolution". Another good example, also in Nigeria, was when General Babangida's regime overthrew General Buhari's regime. It abandoned Buhari's program "War Against Indiscipline" or "WAI" even though it was a good program directed at reshaping the society.

Many other better examples abound, however, what should be learnt is that completely scraping valuable programs introduced by previous administrations is a waste of societies' time, money and energy or resources. Also, it retards progress and/or development within the society.

With the doctrine of Incrementalism, governments should learn to continue whatever good-spirited programs any previous administration may have initiated for the commonweal. It suffices to say: it saves time, money, effort, and exacerbates growth in terms of development.

Responsiveness

The term responsiveness could be defined as the promptitude with which a government or agency responds to problems, suggestions, appeals, or demands for policy change. "Responsiveness can also mean that the government does more than merely react to popular demands. In some cases, it can mean that government takes initiatives in the proposal of solutions for problems and even in the definition of problems."[102]

Governmental responsiveness can transcend national boundaries for instance, the promptitude with which the United States and its allies intervened in Sedam Hussain's entanglement with Saudi Arabia is a good exemplification of governmental responsiveness at international level. Also, Nigeria's February 13, 1998 effective ousting of the Sierra Leone's military junta, Maj. Paul Koroma, and reinstalling the democratically elected government of Ahmed Tejan Kabbah, is another good example of (international) governmental responsiveness. Be that as it may, this example is also a paradox, if not a mockery of the precept of governmental responsiveness. Nations should practice what they preach. Nigeria which wallows under militarism should first practice democracy before it advocates the same for its neighbors.

The readiness to tackle the socio-economic problems facing the nation, which characterizes the Indian Congress Party, is a good example of governmental responsiveness. In most Third World nations, however, the government is either slow, or in some cases non-responsive, in certain national or local issues of great import. For instance, in some West African nations, the government does not deem it a governmental responsibility to provide or create jobs for its citizens. The contrary is the case in advanced nations where the government aids in that regard. For instance, in the United States, the Atlanta journal: The Atlanta Constitution, of July 6, 1996 revealed how 239,000 jobs were created in May of 1996 alone.

Nor does the government in Third World nations see it as its responsibility to take care of the elderly via social security, or the sick via Medicare/Medicaid or a replica of those services as exist in advanced countries.

Also, in some Third World nations, particularly in big cities, a copse could be found every now and then, decaying and unattended to. In such instances, the government is unresponsive and, perhaps, doesn't see it as its duty to take care of such unidentified and/or unclaimed corpse. It stays there, till the dead buries itself. Is such a government responsive? No. A thousand times no.

In the United States, in the aftermath of Rodney King's beatings and the rioting in Los Angeles following the court's verdict, the government as in many other issues of social concern promptly investigated the problem and took necessary legislative action to prevent the occurrence of similar human-rights violation. That could be seen as another exemplification of governmental responsiveness; and so is the immediate action taken by the US government soon after the Valu-Jet crash in the Everglades.

Dereliction of duty is what is obtainable in most Third World nations wherein, the police and other governmental officials merely turn the other way. Take for instance, in fighting armed bandits. In most of the Third World nations, the police do not even go to the scene to quell the corruption. Most of the time, the police only go to the scene after the robbers may have finished their business and gone. This is governmental unresponsiveness. In the Third World nations in general and Africa in particular, what we need is governmental responsiveness.

In sum, responsiveness is the yardstick with which to measure how quick a government reacts to the problems facing a nation in social, political, economic and other concerns.

Competence

Competence in this account, encompasses how a country uses its resources - human, natural, financial, industrial, technological, political and social. In this regard, a nation or its applicable agency could be seen as being competent if it manages its programs well – to effectuate desired positive results in uplifting societal wellness.

A look at the sort of services obtainable at the hospitals in our nations could reveal whether or not the hospital administration in such a society is competent. In most Third World countries, it is not uncommon to notice that many hospitals do not have ambulances nor are they well equipped to handle emergencies. In some places where the equipment and ambulances are available, efficient and effective services are still encumbered by bad and/or poor road conditions. In such a case, it would take unusually too long for the ambulances to render, even, minimal services.

In the same regard, many Third World nations lack efficient fire services. Yet, in some others, fire trucks exist only on paper or in their dreams. In the very few places where they actually exist, bad roads hinder timely services. Worst still, should the fire trucks arrive at the scenes, there are mostly no fire hydrants or the availability of any reliable pipe-borne water system to facilitate fire-fighting.

There are many other better examples with which to measure how competent the government of a nation and the subsidiary agencies operate. The examples given above are sufficient to intimate a passive observer to social policies on how functional (active or inactive) a particular government is. But, ex abundanti cautela, I may add another one.

In most Third World nations communication systems, especially telephone services, are more or less dysfunctional. More often than not, it would be easier for a camel to pass through the eye of a needle than to place a successful call to the police, the hospital, the firehouse, or a business call.

Governmental incompetence in one area has a chain-reaction or domino-affect in other areas, directly or indirectly. For instance, lack of good roads encumber smooth running of ambulances, etc., which in turn magnify mortality rates. Also, bad roads and bad communication systems retard easy-flow of commerce and may obfuscate economic growth.

Greed

For the purpose of this work, the term greed could be defined as the excessive desire to milk and bilk governmental resources for personal or selfish ends. It is a gluttonous desire for personal financial or material aggrandizement. It is the desire to reap where one did not sow; or the desire to convert public wealth to personal instrument. Finally, it is the desire to amass (personal) fortune at public expense.

In most nations where the activities of government officials are not easily probed, there may be a tendency for greedy officials to amass personal wealth, in millions or billions, starched away in secret bank accounts. The case of Raul Salinas, as mentioned in Chapter Four had just come under review.

Mexico is not the only nation suffering the ailment of greed. It exists in most of our nations, covertly or overtly. Grover Starling alluded to "Influence peddling and political favoritism", wherein An army of lawyers, lobbyists, former members of Congress, and presidential appointees derive handsome incomes from trading on their access to upper levels of government, as greed.[103] While I agree that some leaders, even of advanced nations, are not immune from greed, I do not see "influence peddling and political favoritism" as greed. They are what they are; Favoritism (and/or Nepotism - if a relative is involved in the dispensation, or acceptance of the favor).

The difference between any occurrence taking place in any advanced countries (e.g. the United States) and similar occurrence taking place in a Third World nation (e.g. Vietnam), is that while the former is a country of law not of men, wherein, the law is applied to wo/men and all activities done by anyone even the President could be subjected to scrutiny, in the latter, executive privilege could, perhaps to a greater extent, afford the president an umbrella of protection under which he could act without much if any probe.

Where such is the case, the executive administrator and, perhaps, even their subsidiaries have a greater proclivity to abuse the spirit of greed. In such places, citizens may be enveloped in trepidation for, there is freedom of speech until you speak against the government. Therein, vociferous ones are likely to be at risk of imprisonment and deprivation of their rights and property should they criticize the anomalies as perceived.

To avoid imperilment, individuals may succumb to euphemism or sycophancy. But, things must not be allowed to continue being that way. Honest, vociferous and good-spirited persons should, against all odds, be emboldened to continue agitating.

They should not hesitate to speak their minds and damn the consequences so long as what they are agitating for, in their conscience, is justifiable before God and man, and is for the commonweal. It may take time, it may take imprisonment, and may even take lives, but reform would eventually take place.

When good governance is actualized, to maintain its continuity, the government should from time to time take swift and positive steps to interdict and stamp out any venture or undertaking which could encourage greed and should enjoin or prohibit any venture which is capable of igniting bitterness, and undue and widespread dissatisfaction.

Accountability

Simply put, accountability means amenability, answerability, responsibility, or accountability. It asks that governmental officials or organizations "be answerable to someone or something outside itself. So that, when things go wrong, someone must be held responsible."[104]

Governmental/organizational accountability is very much needed in most Third World nations, to reduce official misconduct, including embezzlements. Although the government of the United States is not immune to official misconduct, the checks and balances amongst the Executive, Legislature and Judiciary is, perhaps, capable of relegating the abuse of power to live only in dreams, at least, for the most part.

In such democratic countries as this, everyone is answerable to someone else – no one is above the law. President Nixon was investigated, and appropriate action taken against him with respect to the Water Gate. In line with this, President Clinton is under investigation for the alleged White Water (scandal). This implies to say that, in a civilized society no one is, and no one should be, above the law.

In light of the above, I applaud the Nigerian government for investigating the actions of ex-president(s), when there is reasonable cause to do so, thereby, planting the seed that no one is above the law; and no preferential treatments (even to ex-presidents) should be allowed.

When a precedence of this magnitude is set, the society is very much en route to accountability.

CHAPTER FOURTEEN

As It Was In the Beginning

As it was in the beginning, so it is, will it remain the same world without end?

When I was a kid, African nations were referred to as underdeveloped (or developing) nations. That was many, many years ago. Today, our nations are still referred to as "developing" or "under-developed" or "undeveloped"; same as it was many, many, years ago. Shall we wear that label till the end of time? Or shall ours grow (economically, socially, and politically) and join the rank and file of developed nations?

We are at a cross-road and it is left for us to choose which direction to follow.

The road is bifurcated. One leads to industrialization, political stability, economic opulence and social development. The other leads to underdevelopment, political instability, economic backwardness, filth and other social vices. We are faced with these two options (or more), though I am not the Speaker of the people, I recommend we tread the road which leads to economic opulence. Only there shall we find a complete stableness in all of life's endeavors. The other roads, in my opinion, would only lead to individualistic, self-gratification; which would last only temporarily.

Kaleidoscopically speaking, Africa is endowed with all the resources with which we can augment the status of our infrastructure. It perplexes me as to why we still lag behind in development. For instance, Nigeria, which is even more developed than most African nations had had electricity in Lagos since 1896 (one hundred years ago), but as of 1984 (and perhaps till this day), not all parts of the country has gotten electricity; nor is there steady power supply in Nigeria, especially at Aba and other southern cities and villages. Frequent power outage has been the norm. If electricity is taking a walk from Lagos to the hinterland, a hundred years of slow-but-steady pace is enough for it to have reached every home in that country. On the same footing, pipe-borne water was introduced in 1913. Till today, it is still a very rare commodity in our midst; eighty-four years is enough to have an efficient and effective water-running system. If these things were made available during the colonial system which we repudiated, shouldn't the indigenous administrators make those essential materials ubiquitously available for us to improve our lives with? Is it too much to ask for the fundamental necessaries to make life moderately comfortable? Having undergone much excruciating crucibles of life, I believe we, as good citizens of our nations should demand, without apologies, that those life-necessities be provided for us. It is our birthright; we have to make such assertions without obfuscation. If nature had not blessed us with a concourse of mineral resources, one could say: well, we cannot have those things because we are poor. If nature (and/or God) had meant for us to be so starved, we would not have been so blessed and endowed.

Look all around our nations. There is not an African nation not superabundantly gifted with more than one mineral. Why then should we not have good educational institutions? Why then may we not have two or three, nourishing, square meals a day? Yet in spite of all these natural advantages (such as diamond, zinc, tin, bauxite, columbium, uranium, plutonium, ore, diatomite, coal, lignite, antimony, etc., etc., etc., which our nations have superfluously in commercial quantities), we are still economically disadvantaged. A genius is not yet born, who could transform our nations from underdeveloped to developed nations by mere magic wands. We have to use what we have, to achieve what we want. This can only be done when we use our resources wisely to the beneficial effect of our respective nations. We have to provide jobs in our nations, for the citizens of our nations. We have to have a solid infrastructural base.

Efficient and effective social amenities are necessary ingredients for a functional society. For example, good tele-communication network, good roads, hospitals, fire-service, transportation systems, dedicated and incorruptible civil service, and police, efficient postal system, and what have you; all these, and more, must we have in our milieus before we even begin to think: we are 'developing' nations. Without these, we are imbibing ourselves with nothing short of delusions. If we cannot achieve the status of 'developed' nationhood now that we still have bountiful resources, when shall we acquire such a status? Resources do not flow forever. They get depleted. What will be our economic lot, when we no longer have any of these natural mineral resources?

Nigeria is one of the biggest suppliers of petroleum to the metropolitan countries, yet, June 1995 (as in many other years) fuel scarcity left cars and other vehicles lined-up for more than two to three miles at a stretch. It makes me wonder how a farmer or a fisherman could starve of his own product. However, it must be mentioned here, that while there is frequent fuel shortage in the South (where petroleum is produced), it is enjoyed more in the North (where it is abundantly made available, through underground tunnel or pipe-line, which runs from Port-Harcourt, in the South, all the way to Kaduna, in the North). It makes me wonder, since it is a national resource, shouldn't all the citizens enjoy it equitably? Must one part of the country enjoy a national privilege more than another part?

The same goes for education. Also in Nigeria, while most states in the federation, especially in the North and the West, enjoy free education (tuition-free, that is), in the South, one pays one's way from Kindergarten to University level. Ethnic quota system has been instituted in the admission procedures into the nation's Universities, whereby some ethnic groups considered to be less educationally advantaged' are given preferential treatment, to some degree, over others. The same is the case in good paved roads. While some good paved roads exist in the South, much more is enjoyed in the North. What justice is there in a nation wherein one segment of the populace receives more favorable treatment than another stratus? Isn't what is good for the goose also good for the gander?

As recently as the end of April, 1996, or thereabouts, the Federal Government of Nigeria banned lots of business centers. Perhaps, the Government was acting under "Decree code 419" to prevent certain indiscernible illegal activities. If this is the case, isn't the police capable of tracking down the illegitimate ones and dealing with them accordingly, while the legitimate ones should be let to function and operate? Should the government close both the good ones and the bad ones all alike? It makes me wonder, shouldn't the government be encouraging, and promoting free-enterprise, rather than stifling such ambition? Or, perhaps, the business centers were closed down to prevent the entrepreneurs from taking telecommunication businesses away from the NITEL (Nigerian Tele-Communications Network) which is a government agency and in an effort to boost its revenue. Whatever the case may be, one has to look at it from a critical standpoint. The proscription of privately owned enterprises which may have direct or indirect competitive ability with a governmental agency does not promote efficiency, nor does it promote economic growth. Besides, it stifles the spirit of entrepreneurship as one may be fearful and less inclined to start a business which may attract (governmental) proscription. The United States of America, for instance, encourages small businesses, and such accounts for more than seventy-five per cent source of employment for Americans. Competition promotes efficiency, while monopoly kills it. As there is more than fifty per cent unemployment ravaging that nation, jobs should be created, not banned. The modus operandi of African (and other Third World) nations should be free-enterprise, and encouragement of small businesses. Anything short of that is directly or indirectly relegating our nations to the prehistoric age.

If for anything, joblessness promotes ill-will and social vices such as prostitution, robbery, anger, petite and grand frauds as well as some other unscrupulous acts. One may mention here, perhaps in parenthesis, that an argument might be interposed that prostitution is not a big deal; after all, it is the oldest profession.

By the way, is prostitution really the oldest profession in the world? Absolutely not. The oldest profession in the world is Agriculture. According to the Scriptures (Genesis), when God created man, he was created alone (thus, Adam was alone and could not have copulated), then he was given charge over all livestock: birds of the air, fish of the sea, and all the creatures that move on the ground, and all the trees of the garden (except one).

That one exception was only violated long after the creation of Eve. Eve could not have done the copulation before she was introduced, nor could Adam have done it alone. If the serpent did it, did he really pay for it? If he didn't, then, it cannot be called prostitution. But, even if he did, it was ex post facto (i.e. after the fact, or long after) Adam had been assigned to man the garden. It suffices therefore to say that Adam was busy with this first profession, Agriculture, before the creation of woman, and therefore, before the eating of the "fruit".

It is unfortunate however, that this oldest profession (perhaps due to its old age) has suffered a great deal of neglect. Lots of our youngsters shy away from it.

But, serendipitously, our youths will rediscover the treasure of this profession; nevertheless, they first have to be encouraged; most probably through government subsidies and humanitarian aids.

It has been mentioned above, that joblessness introduces social vices. On the other hand, the creation of jobs is an avenue through which self-confidence could be created. Jobs would give the people the opportunity to master their own fate, and control their own destinies.

However, it is unfortunate that most governments of the Third World countries are more or less incorrigible and would proffer to censure any public opinion and/or criticism contrary to praise-singing. They do not accept anything but sycophancy. In most of these countries, criticizing unpopular government actions is putting one's life in peril. For instance, in Dahomey, one must cherish and support. If one doesn't, then one's "life is in danger."[105] Usually, the advice given by friends and well-wishers is for one to be wary in criticizing the government, to avoid putting oneself in jeopardy. Even, one does not have to be careful with only the government, one has to also be wary of friendly-enemies (those who pretend to be your friends, but in reality they hate you and whatever little progress you may have made; i.e. the lions in sheep's clothing), also, one is circumspect of the jealous and callous persons. Even the way you talk, or conduct yourself, is enough to net you a score of enemies. In most African countries much like in Dahomey, "people feel insulted if they have to watch a kinsman or neighbour doing better than the average...They take it out of him... This may sound strange to you, but...he really does lose his right to live."[106] Otherwise, if one finds the means of controlling oneself to avoid unnecessary mishaps, he becomes ostracized, and "he can never become a proper member of the kindred again." This will force him "to grow a shell of individualism, under which his new...interior life can shelter." Then, he "invokes modem values as a defence against the importunities of his kin-group." The next alternative he may have is to escape abroad which in itself is equivalent to self imposed exile. But if "he fails to escape abroad into physical exile, he falls back on this spiritual exile that he struggles to impose on himself at home. It's the most painful of all kinds of division from his own people."[107]

Sometimes, the enemies may "take out a subscription with the witch-doctors;" and use "the old practices of sorcery" to "threaten him. Make no mistake about that. The fetish-merchants can literally create a cloud of hatred and jealousy under which man and man, village and village, may tear one another to pieces."[108] All these are the problems which may face a person determined to live an honest, peaceful, prosperous, and law-abiding life in his community. This is the case, not just in Dahomey, but, in most Third World nations, including, but not limited to, West African countries.

It behooves me to ask: What does it profit a man, to have strove to better himself and his community, in all and any legitimate fashion, only to suffer persecution and, perhaps, the loss of his own life? Should one abrogate the tenet of one's moral foundation (honesty) and join the crowd, in order to save oneself from any imperil? In my opinion, taking this format is tantamount to choosing to live in a 'state of nature' where life is insecure; therein, the survival of the fittest overtakes the life of the meek and the humble. In such a society, security is at issue. And such is the case in our societies. The weaker is always at the capricious mercy of the stronger. Thus, for the most part, danger is almost always unavoidable, hi some instances, "it is possible for an African to make 'medicine' so that another African may go blind, or insane, or dead." In the same vein, "an African standing five hundred yards away or more may make 'medicine' to kill his fellow African. Granting that this is possible, the African scientist" first ascertains "what form the 'medicine' would take. Could it be solid? No. Because the African did not wish his victim to see him. Could it be liquid? No. Because it is not possible to do so, for obvious reasons. Could it be gaseous? Probably so, but would not contact with the air neutralize the gas and make it to dissolve in the atmosphere?" Probably not. However, although this is difficult to believe, for lack of scientific proof, it is an empirical fact. And, "unless the African scientist could invent forth a form or nature of matter which is unknown in the realm of pure science, whatever conclusions he had built up on the bases of his theories of 'medicine' must fall flat. This does not mean that it is not true. It is simply this: That this brand of African 'medicine' is demonstrable."[109]

But, why should anyone have the inclination to destroy another out of callousness and jealousy? What claim does anyone have on anyone's life; as to desire so seriously to terminate the life no one knows how it came to be nor does anyone know where it ends?

Indeed, "human nature is so remarkable that its make-up is still unfathomable. One may orate on certain phases of human nature. One may theorize on other phases of it, but in the final analysis it is impossible to make a categorical statement as to what constitutes human nature.

At one time, human nature becomes an easy task for the quack - say the physiognomist, the mesmerist, the hypnotist, the palmist, the fortune-teller, etc., but when it comes to a showdown, none, not even the scientifically trained psychologist, can explain, without reservation, the constitution of human nature."[110] This being the case, shouldn't we join hands with each other and progress in unison; otherwise, leave each other alone to live to the fullest manifestation of each other's individual destiny?

Shouldn't we proffer a society based on honesty, fear-free, prosperous and progressive? When the Pan-Africanists and the apostles of African

Nationalism showed us the light, they had meant for all of us to toe the line and partake in the titanic struggle for the freedom of all Africa from exploitation in every form. They had meant for us to participate in creating a hate-free, fear-free and a greed-free continent peopled by free men and women. Here, the phrase 'free1, is quite unambiguous. Quixotically, the fathers of our independence had meant for us to actualize the maximum happiness (freedom) through our personal and collective endeavours. They had meant for us to socially, politically, and economically better ourselves, individually, collectively, and nationally (to the best of our abilities).

By this, shouldn't the jealous and callous ones struggle in all legitimate ways permissible by law, to better themselves, so that in the end, we all would be one prosperous, happy community? Because, to live in fear is analogous to living in slavery, and to live in economic squalor (for fear of attracting jealousy and callousness from neighbours) is equivalent to living in chains.

Whatever may be the case, one must not cower. One must find a way to improve the situation. As a memento, one should always bear in mind that all it requires to effectuate a positive change in self and in society is understanding and relentless development. No matter what.

Despite this, the only other alternative whereby one can have any peace is by going into physical or spiritual exile; living abroad for most (if not all) of one's productive life. Is life so dear, or peace so sweet, as to be purchased at the price of cowardice and remain in economic thraldom and socio-political undevelopment? Forbid it, Almighty God! I know not what course others may take; but as for me, give me economic liberty or give me death!

As long as one is performing one's civic duties, being honest to oneself and to the Almighty God to the best of one's abilities, one should not be afraid of those who can destroy the flesh but cannot harm the soul So be it Lord, as long as what one is doing is upright and, in one's opinion can lead to the betterment of the society, one has to pursue that course; without fear or intimidation.

Be it as it may, our governments should learn to put public opinion to their profitable spell. How else can the governments know what is going wrong in the societies, without making use of unbiased public opinion polls and constructive criticisms? While it is wrong, uncanny, uncivil and seditious to inveigh one's government with infamous lampoons, it must be stated that, honest, unbiased, well-founded criticisms are a vehicle through which amends are made. Therefore, in my opinion, governments should use this medium efficiently, and should not persecute those that produce it, so long as the criticisms are well-founded, and not baseless.

As Africa was in the beginning, so it is, and shall (not) remain so, for ever and ever. I hope and pray, it has to change. Every continent is socially moving. While others' are making a forward movement, ours is making a backward movement. Although they are all movements of some sort, a progressive movement is what we vie for, not a retrogressive one. Unfortunately, however, what we have is a retrogressive movement while other continents, more or less, have a progressive movement. The natural resources within our spell, in my opinion, should be effectively and efficiently used to produce the development needed in our nations. If we are having so many problems now that we still have the resources, what will be the fate of our respective nations in particular and African continent in general, when the resources stop flowing? If we cannot use our resources in a more beneficial way, to produce a brighter future for African children, what will be their fate and the fate of their posterity, say fifty-to-a-hundred years from now? Should we be so myopic, so greedy, so callous, and so nonchalant not to think that far? Knowing that Africa belongs not just to us, but to the future generations shall we be happy, when we may have been gone, to look down from heaven and see our children and their generations scorching, toiling, and wallowing in poverty which we may have engendered them to; through our actions, omissions and commissions? It may have been late (too late indeed) for our generation to hope to see a developed Africa, but, it is our steadfast obligation, from ethical and moral standpoint, to pave the way for the posterity of Africa, to enable them have a sublime economic condition, better that what we have had. Thus, the future of Africa's children is in our hands; the foundation we lay for them now, through development, would be solid panoply for them against bad times. For this, we dare not extinguish the flame of development.

We have to keep it alit. For this, let us pray:

Our fathers who are in Heaven, glory be your names for the works you have done.

You are now resting in heaven after your mighty works on earth. May you intercede for us before the Almighty God, that He may accord us the wisdom to discern good from evil. That He may guide us to the pathway of economic sovereignty.

You fought immeasurable intellectual battles to bring us political independence; may you pray for us that the Source of Wisdom may enlighten our minds to know that political independence is only a channel to economic independence without which all is a vanity.

May you assist in channeling our prayers to the Mighty One, and ask that He refurbishes our strengths and grant us the fortitude with which to continue the good work you commenced.

May you always join hands with our glorious ancestors to defend us from political blunders and socioeconomic calamities. Guide and protect us from fumbling. Due to the foibles of humanity, if we should stumble and fall during the course of our race toward a better political economy, accord us the wisdom not to take it personal. Teach us to learn from past mistakes. Teach us that in political races there are no losers, only scholars; teach us how to get back in such races; how to improve our national lots; and, how to do for our nations and continent what others have done for theirs.

May you pray for us that the Almighty Father may adorn us with altruistic spirit which will make us do for the community and the nation at large rather than being self-centered; that He may take away from us the spirit of selfishness, atomism, tribalism, sectionalism, racial-sentimentalism, betrayal, avariciousness, self-righteousness, egoism, or any other evil spirit that would induce one to enrich oneself at the expense of others.

You and our good-spirited ancestors "brought us Young Africans, into this world. You played your part from a biological point of view.

God blessed your role and so we came into this world, just as you and your ancestors did.

It was not your intention to make our lot a hard and severe one. Yours was a noble philosophy of life – to make life worthwhile for your children so that they might enjoy life more abundantly.

It was not your motive to make our fate comparable to that of a slave whose future is blighted by the chains around his feet and his hands and his neck.

Rather, you desired a better world for us. You desired better conditions for us so that we might improve, at least one whit better than you did in your days.

Allow us to assume, fathers, that you realized the incorrigibility of human nature, and that was why you made up your minds to do all you could to make life less tedious for us.

You also realized our innocence. You knew that as children we were immature in thinking. You knew that we could be advised to accept certain opinions and to form certain habits.

These, you understood to have a bearing on our character, yet you insisted that we should condition our flexes and thinking apparatuses to them.

Now, dignified fathers, we are grown up, and we look forward to the better life which you have promised us, and behold our lot is far from being satisfactory.

Instead of economic security, we are faced with the hyena which howls and growls and threatens our very existence.

Instead of social security, we are faced with divisions and tribal prejudices which make it impossible for us, your children, to work together in harmony.

Instead of political security, we are faced with an era which goes back into the early beginnings of history of worshippers of Democracy,' (and military politicians) 'who had to fight and grumble and complain where they could enjoy their rightful heritage.

Instead of religious security, we are faced with divisions based on dogmas which affect our very philosophy of life, because they make us regard our colleagues as different from us.

Abba, when you brought us into the world, did you foresee these socionomic cataclysms? Were you apprehensive that ours would be a lot of servitude and social disruption? And now that we are in the milieu of social, economic and political catastrophes, and we look forward to you to extricate us, since you are responsible for our habit formations and character, are we wrong in asking you to save yourselves also from this difficulty? What heritage did your fathers leave you? What heritage do you propose to leave to us? And what heritage do you suppose we will leave to our children?"[111]

As you and your fathers went through a life of self-sacrifice in order to leave to us a heritage that enabled us have a better life than what you had, may you teach us to be less greedy, and assist us in leaving a heritage to our children and their posterity which will enable them have a much brighter future than what we have.

May you particularly intercede for us before the Almighty Father, and help us quench the fires of sectional interests, of personal greed and ambition among leaders and contesting aspirants to power. These we ask of you in unity with the Holy Spirit, Oh! Mighty fathers, for ever and ever. Make no mistake about it, because our problems are many, a long prayer such as this, is necessary to attract the needed attention of our forefathers and the glorious Divine intervention.

SUMMARY

Since the beginning of time Africa has undergone one aspect of subjugation and suppression to another. The physical and psychological effects are still being felt within the continent and to some degree even beyond. Physically, the natural resources (in terms of human and material resources still being) siphoned from that continent is hindering economic growth and stultifying what purports to be industrial development. Psychologically, the Africans' continual belief in the superiority and inferiority of one race over another is having a deleterious effect on the Africans. It is time the people extricated themselves from that quagmire of mental chasms. It is time they had self-confidence in themselves, thereby, forging ahead to carve themselves a place in the sun and make their footprints in the sand of time.

The people must also, through their leaders, stamp out the autocratic paternalism of colonialism which is bureaucratic in form and regionalistic or tribalistic in policy, it suppresses initiative, creativity or the spirit of inventiveness. Our governments should support, and subsidize our indigenous engineers, inventors, contractors, agriculturists, etc. The poverty that eclipses and ravages our nations can slowly but progressively be reduced by embarking on relentless economic productivity and result-oriented industrialization. When that sleeping giant awakens, and the heights of developments are attained in areas of science, technology, industry, politics and economics, it would be fair to boldly and justifiably claim that *on qui n'a pas été en Afrique n'a pas été au paradis; ce qui est la même chose que dire: celui qui n'a pas été au Afrique n'ira pas au paradise* (one who has not been to Africa has not been to paradise).

BIBLIOGRAPHY

Abraham, W. E. The Mind of Africa, The University of Chicago Press, 1962.

Achunike, H C, Dreams of Heaven: A Modern Response to Christianity. In North-Western Igboland, 1970-1990, Enugu: Snaap Press, 1995.

Afigbo, A E, The Making of Modern Africa: Volume 1 The Nineteenth Century, Hong Kong: Longman, 1986.

Aristotle, Politics and Poetics, USA: Viking Colonial Press, 1957.

Awolowo, O., Path to Nigerian Federalism, London: Faber Press, 1947.

Azikiwe, N. Renascent Africa, London: Frank Cass, 1937,1968.

Azikiwe, N A Selection from the Speeches of Nnamdi Azikiwe, England: Cambridge University Press, 1961.

Barnes, L., African Renaissance, Great Britain: Bobbs-Merrill Press, 1969.

Carter, G. M. Nationalism in Eight African States, New York: Cornell University Press, 1966.

Chinweizu, Decolonising the African Mind, London: Pero Press, 1987.

Ferkiss, V. C. Africa's Search For Identity, New York: George Braziller Press, 1966.

Freund, B., The Making Of Contemporary Africa: The Development of African Society since 1800, Bloomington: Indiana University Press, 1984.

Gutteridge, W.F. Military Regimes In Africa, London: Methuen Ltd., 1975.

Harbeson, J. Africa in World Politics: Post-Cold War Challenges, San Francisco: Westview Press, 1995.

Harris, P. B., Studies In African Politics, London: Hutchinson Press, 1970.

Harrison, P. Inside The Third World: We Wand Bread Not Cake, Great Britain: Penguin Press, 1982.

Hodgkin, T. Nationalism in Colonial Africa, New York University Press, 1957.

Legura, C. Pan-Africanism: A short Political Guide, Frederick Praeger Press, New York, 1965.

Locke, J., The Second Treatise On Civil Government, New York: Prometheus, 1986.

Marcuse, H. One-Dimensional Man, Beacon Press, 1964.

Mazrui, A. A., Nationalism and New States in Africa: from about 1935 to present, London: Heinemann Educational Press, 1984.

Nkrumah, K., Africa Must Unite, New York: International Press, 1963.

Nnoli, O., Ethnic Politics In Nigeria, Enugu: Fourth Dimension Press, 1980.

Ojiako, J.O., Nigeria: Yesterday, Today, And...?, Onitsha: African Educational Press, 1981.

Okpoko, J., The Biafran Nightmare: The Controversial Role of International Relief Agencies In a War of Genocide, Enugu: Delta Press, 1986.

Onwubiko, K. B. C., History of West Africa 1800-Present Day, Aba: African Educational Press, 1973.

Padmore, G., Africa: Britain's Third Empire, Negro Universities Press, 1969.

Ritner, P., The Death of Africa, New York: The Macmillan Press, 1960.

Rodney, W., Walter Rodney Speaks: The Making of an African Intellectual, New Jersey: Africa World Press, 1990.

Scribner, C., Africa Independent: A Survey of Political Developments, New York: Keesing's Publications, 1972.

Stepan, A., Rethinking Military Politics: Brazil and the Southern Cone, Princeton University Press, 1988.

Wallbank, T. W., Contemporary Africa: Continent In Transition, New York: D. Van Nostrand Press, 1956.

Wallerstein, I. Africa: The Politics Of Independence, New York: Random House, 1961.

Weinstein W. The Pattern of African Decolonization: A New Interpretation, New, York: Syracuse University, 1973.

INDEX

J

Jacobs Eliza Capitein- 20
Jealousy and Callousness- 207
Jesus Christ- 28, 35
Jewish God- 25
Jimmy Carter- 127
John F. Kennedy- 53, 139
John the Baptist- 137
Jomo Kenyatta of Kenya- 88
Jones, W. S. (1985)
Nationalism- 165
Joseph B. Danquah- 89
Joseph Danquah- 92
Judgement- 20
Julius Nyerere of Tanzania- 88
Jurisdiction of Ghanaian Courts- 91
Justice AtandaFatayi-Williams- 122
Justice B. O. Kazeem- 121

K

Kabaka of Bugandi- 95
Kaleidoscopically- 36
Kenneth Kaunda of Zambia- 88
Kin-Group- 205
Kwame Nkrumah of Ghana, see
    also Nkrumah- 52, 56, 88,
    89, 92
Kwashiokor- 109

L

Land-Tenor System- 158
Latin Africa- 53
Latin America- 143
Legum,C(1965)
    Negro African poets,13
Liberia's Mineral Resources- 15
Liberian Mining Company- 15

Life-Blood of a Nation- 188
Lord Hailey- 47
Lord Lugard- 15
Lt Col Oliver North- 114
Lt Colonel Chukwuemeka
    Odumegwu Ojukwu- 104
Lt Colonel Yakubu Gowon- 104
Lucifer (Black)- 28, 30
Macro Identification- 163
Made in England- 41
    IBO Coinage- 42

M

Major Anthony Ochefu- 167
Major ChukwuaNzeogwu- 104
Major General Collin Powell- 114
Major Paul Koroma- 193
Manchester Guardian- 58
Marcus Garvey- 13, 79, 81, 82
Marcuse, H (1964)
Commonwealth- 160
Margaret Thatcher- 127
Martin Luther- 35
Mass Literacy- 174
Material Aggrandizement- 196
Mau Mau in Kenya- 112
Mazrui, A. A. & Tidy, M. (1984)
    Liberia,s mineral resources, 15
    Northern Rhodesia,15
Political Profiteers- 107
Media of Communication- 36
Mental and Psychological
    Surgery- 166
Mental Emancipation- 166, 172
Mental Servitude- 86
Mercantilism- 40
Metropolitan-39
    Administration- 37, 57, 58

Nigeria, Cocoa- 15
Nigerian Labour Congress- 63
Nigerian-Biafran Civil War- 29
Nkrumah, Kwame (1963)
Balkan Peninsula,53
Neo-colonized states,56,60
Hill,R&Dodsonj H.(1990)
Producing quality goods,40
Positive Changes- 144
Nkrumah, Ghana- 131
Nkrumah's Despotic
Government- 124
Nkrumah's Philosophy- 56
Nkrumahism- 94, 191
NnamdiAzikiwe of Nigeria- 52, 88
Nnewi - 120
Nnoli, O. (1978)
Nationalism- 164
Non-Tribal Western Societies- 47

O

Obafemi Awolowo of Nigeria-
70, 88
Obasanjo O(1987)
Debt,62
Military Regime- 192
Obasi-Igwe- 24
Obete, Ugada- 131
Odomankoma- 26
Ogbu-nigwe- 180
Ojiako, J. O. (1981)
MelfordOkilo- 122
Ojukwu's Biafra- 189
Ojukwu-Catapult- 180
Okpensi- 33
Okpoko, J. (1986)
Nigerian Civil War- 110

Old Testament of the Bible- 23,
34, 38,
Oligarchic Government- 134
Oligarchical Government- 132
Oligarchical Parties- 132, 133, 133
Olisa- 24
One-Party State- 92
Onwubuiko,K. B. C(1973)
Colonial power,37
Operation Feed the Nation- 192
Opprobrious Stigma- 87, 178
Organizational Accountability- 198
Otumfuo the Mightiest- 26
Overzealous Military- 106

P

Paganish- 32
Pagans- 28
Palmist- 207
Pan-Africanists- 81, 207
Panama Canal-Zone- 53
Parsimoniousness- 134
PartiDemocratique de Guinee
(PDG)- 98
PartidoRevolucionario Institutional
(Revolutionary Party)- 132
Paternalism of Colonialism- 214
Paternalistic and Magical word- 99
Patriotism- 165
Personal Accountability- 38
Petroleum- 8
Philosophy of Life- 211
Physiognomist- 207
Pipe-Borne Water- 200
Platinum- 16
Policy- 111
Policy Mismanagement- 61
Political Profiteers- 107

188

ENDNOTES

[1]   Nnamdi Azikiwe, Zik: A Selection from the Speeches of Nnamdi Azikiwe (London: Cambridge, 1961) 61.

[2]   Aristotle, Politics & Poetics (USA: Viking, 1952) 28.

[3]   A.E. Afigbo, E.A. Ayandele, et. al, The Making of Modern Africa (Hong Kong: Longman, 1987) 91.

[4]   Immanuel Wallerstein, Africa: The Politics of Independence (New York: Vintage, 1961) 16.

[5]   Colin Legum, Pan-Africanism (New York: Frederick Praeger Press, 1965)95.

[6]   AH A. Mazrui et. al., Nationalism and New States in Africa (Great Britain: Richard clay, 1984) 38.

[7]   Ibid., 39.

[8]   W. E. Abraham, The Mind of Africa (Chicago: The University of Chicago, 1962), 124.

[9]   Ibid.

[10] Ibid., 122-3.

[11] Ibid., 120.

[12] Ibid, 118.

[13] Ibid., 137.

[14] K. B. C. Onwubiko, History Of West Africa: Book Two 1800-Present Day (Aba: African Educational Press, 1973)253

[15] W. E. Abraham, The Mind Of Africa (Chicago: The University of Chicago, 1962), 136.

[16] Kwame Nkruma, Africa Must Unite (New York: International Press, 1963) xiv.

[17] Hilary C. Achunike, Dreams of Heaven: Modern Response to Christianity in North-Western Igboland, 1970-1990 (Enugu: Snaap Press, 1995) 7.

[18] Peter Ritner, The Death of Africa (New York: Macmillan, 1960)213.

19 P. B. Harris, Studies in African Politics (London: Hutchinson, 1970) 36.

20 W. F. Gutteridge, Military Regimes In Africa (London: Methuen Press, 1975) 23.

21 Nnamdi Azikiwe, Renascent Africa (London: Frank Cass, 1968) 141.

22 Chinweizu, Decolonising the African Mind (Lagos, Nigeria: Pero, 1987)39.

23 Kwame Nkruma, Africa Must Unite (New York: International Press, 1963) 173.

24 Chinweizu, Decolonising the African Mind (Lagos, Nigeria: Pero Press, 1987) 31.

25 Kwame Nkrumah, Africa Must Unite (New York: International Press, 1963) 174.

26 Robert Hill & Howard Dodson, Walter Rodney Speaks: The Making of an African Intellectual (Trenton, New Jersey: Africa World Press, 1990) 34.

27 T. Walter Wallbank, Contemporary Africa: Continent in Transition (1956; Princeton, New Jersey: D. VanNostrand Company, Inc. 1964) 65.

28 Jan Black, Latin America, Its Problems and Its Promise (Boulder, Colorado, USA: Westview Press, 1984)55.

29 Kwame Nkruma, Africa Must Unite (New York: International Press, 1963) 174.

30 W. F. Gutteridge, Military Regimes in Africa (London: Methuen, 1975) 73.

31 Olusegun Obasanjo, Africa In Perspective: Myths and Realities (New York: Council on Foreign Relations, 1987) 22.

32 Chinweizu, Decolonizing the African Mind (Lagos, Nigeria: Pero Press, 1987) 53.

33 Ibid., 38.

34 Ibid., 45

35 Ibid., 40.

36 Ibid., 100.

37 Ibid., 100-1.

38 Obafemi Awolowo, Path to Nigerian Freedom (London: Faber, 1947) 49.

39 Leonard Barnes, African Renaissance (Great Britain: Bobbs-Morril, 1969) 115.

40 Chinweizu, Decolonising the African Mind (Great Britain: Pero Press, 1987) 101.

41 Ibid., 139-140.

[42] Marcus Garvey, Philosophy and Opinions (Vol.2) (New York: Atheneum, 1974) 13.

[43] Ibid., 416.

[44] Ibid., 1974)415-16.

[45] Chinweizu, Decolonising the African Mind (Lagos, Nigeria: Pero, 1987) 159.

[46] Ibid., 31.

[47] Nnamdi Azikiwe, Renascent Africa (London: Frank Cass, 1968)164.

[48] Ibid.

[49] Ibid., 165-6.

[50] Immanuel Wallerstein, Africa: The politics of Independence (New York: Vintage, 1961) 64.

[51] Hilary Achunike, Dreams of Heaven: A Modern Response to Christianity in North-Western Igboland, 1970-1990 (Enugu: Snaap, 1995) 21.

[52] Chinweizu, Decolonizing the African Mind (Lagos: Pero, 1987)58.

[53] Ibid.

[54] Ibid.

[55] Ibid.

[56] Ibid. 60.

[57] Ibid., 60-61.

[58] Alfred Stepan, Rethinking Military Politics: Brazil and the Southern Cone (New Jersey: Princeton University Press, 1988) ix.

[59] W. F. Gutteridge, Military Regimes In Africa (London: Methuen, 1975) 1.

[60] Ibid.

[61] Ibid., 6.

[62] A. K. Ocran, A Myth is Broken: An Account of the Ghana Coup d' Etat (London: Publisher, 1968) 26.

[63] W. F. Gutteridge, Military Regimes In Africa (London: Methuen & Co Ltd, 1975) 2.

[64] Charlse Scribner, Africa Independent: A Study of Political Developments (New York: Keesing, 1972) 118.

[65] Ali A. Mazrui & Michael Tidy, Nationalism and New States in Africa (London: Richard Clay, 1984) 249.

[66] Ibid., 239.

[67] Ibid., 239-240.

[68] Charles Scribners, Africa Independent: A study of Political Development (New York: Keesing, 1972) 109.

[69] Ibid., 114.

70   John Okpoko, The Biafran Nightmare (Enugu: Delta Press, 1986)7.
71   Ibid., Ibid., p. 13.
72   S, E. Finer, The Man on Horseback: the Role of the Military in Politics London, 1962.
73   Alfred Stepan, Rethinking Military Politics: Brazil and the Southern Cone (Princeton, New Jersey: Princeton University Press, 1988) 13.
74   Nnamdi Azikiwe, Zik : A Selection from the Speeches of Nnamdi Azikiwe (London: Cambridge, 1961)58-59.
75   James O. Ojiako, Nigeria: Yesterday, Today, and...? (Onitsha, Nigeria: Africana, 1981) 308-9.
76   Ibid., 310.
77   Ibid., 298.
78   W. F. Gutteridge, Military Regimes in Africa (London, 1975)81.
79   Marcus Cunliffe, The Presidency (Boston: Houghton Press, 87) 78.
80   Robert C. Fried, Comperative Political Institutions (New York: Macmillan, 1966) 116-7.
81   Walter Rodney, The Groundings with My Brothers (London: Bogle L'Ouverture, 1969) 16.
82   Chinweizu, Decolonizing the African Mind (Lagos: Pero, 1987)211.
83   Nnamdi Azikiwe, Renascent Africa (London: Frank Cass, 1968)92.
84   Ibid., 95.
85   Jan Black, Latin America: Its Problems and Its promise (Boulder, Colorado, U.S.A: Westview Press, 1984)7.
86   Kwame Nkruma, Africa Must Unite (New York: Intemation Press, 1963) 187.
87   Nnamdi Azikiwe, Renascent Africa (1937; Loud, in Frank Cass, 1968)305-9.
88   Paul Harrison, Inside The Third World (New York: Penguin Press, 1979)21.
89   Ibid. 21-22.
90   Ibid., 31.
91   Ibid., Ibid., p. 24.
92   Ibid., Ibid., p. 287.
93   Aristotle, Politics & Poetics (New York: Viking, 1952) 27.
94   Herbert Marcuse, One Dimensional Man (Boston: Beacon Press, 1964) ix.
95   Okwudiba Nnoli, Ethnic Politics in Nigeria (Enugu, Nigeria: Fourth Dimension, 1978) 176.

[96] Walter S. Jones, The Logic of International Relations (Fifth Edition) (Boston, Mass: Little, 1985)401.

[97] Nnamdi Azikiwe, Renascent Africa (1937; London: Frank Cass, 1968) 17.

[98] Paul Harrison, Inside the Third World (New York: Penguin, 1981)306.

[99] Nnamdi Azikiwe, Renascent Africa (1937: London: Frank Cass, 1968) 25.

[100] Paul Harrison, Inside the Third World (New York: Penguin Press, 1979) 70.

[101] Nnamdi Azikiwe, Zik: A Selection of the Speeches of Nnamdi Azikiwe (London: Cambridge, 1961) 24.

[102] Grover Starling, Managing the Public Sector (Belmont, California: Wadsworth, 1993) 131.

[103] Ibid., 147

[104] Ibid 134

[105] Leonard Barnes, African Renaissance (Great Britain: Boos-Merrill, 1969) 115.

[106] Ibid., 116

[107] Ibid.

[108] Ibid., 116

[109] Nnamdi Azikiwe, Renascent Africa (1937: London: Frank Cass, 1968) 142.

[110] Ibid., 15

[111] Ibid., 39 39 - 40

Printed in the United States
By Bookmasters